# DIY Wardrobe Makeovers

**Alter, Refresh & Refashion Your Clothes** // Step-by-Step Sewing Tutorials

*Suzannah Hamlin Stanley*

stash BOOKS®
an imprint of C&T Publishing

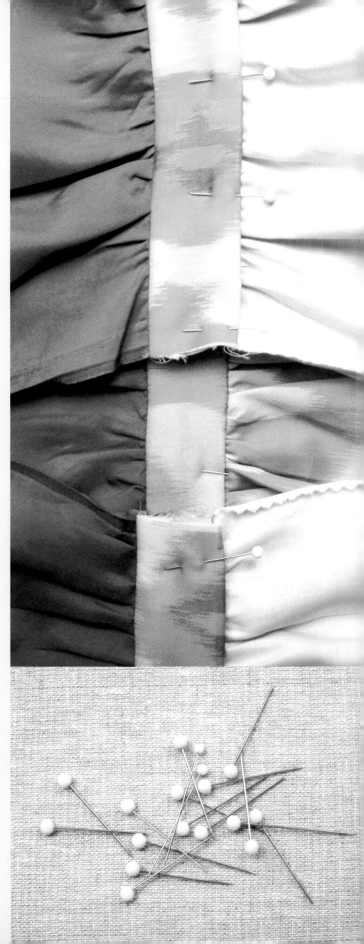

Publisher: Amy Marson

Creative Director: Gailen Runge

Art Director / Book Designer: Kristy Zacharias

Editors: Lynn Koolish and Monica Gyulai

Technical Editors: Mary E. Flynn and Gailen Runge

Production Coordinator: Jenny Davis

Production Editor: Joanna Burgarino

Illustrator: Zinnia Heinzmann

Photo Assistant: Mary Peyton Peppo

Style photography by Nissa Brehmer and instructional photography by Suzannah Hamlin Stanley, unless otherwise noted

Published by Stash Books, an imprint of C&T Publishing, Inc., P.O. Box 1456, Lafayette, CA 94549

Library of Congress Cataloging-in-Publication Data

Stanley, Suzannah Hamlin, 1987-

DIY wardrobe makeovers : alter, refresh & refashion your clothes : step-by-step sewing tutorials / Suzannah Hamlin Stanley.

pages cm

ISBN 978-1-61745-042-6 (soft cover)

1. Clothing and dress--Remaking.  I. Title.

TT550.S73 2015

646'.3--dc23

2014036813

Printed in China

# Contents

# Dedication

This book is dedicated to every reader who doesn't yet realize the power she has to take control and **do it herself!**

# Acknowledgments

I am so grateful for the opportunity to write this book and share my knowledge and passion on paper as well as on my blog. I've spent years practicing, photographing, writing, learning, and teaching what I know and I'm so happy I can bind up my favorite skills and projects in this book. I wouldn't know any of what I know now if it weren't for my talented and inspiring mother, who taught me to sew so many years ago, and whose wealth of knowledge I am still so happy to have available to me when I need it! Massive thanks also go out to my understanding husband, who has been so patient and helpful during the incredible process of writing this book and who, since Day One, has supported whatever goals I pursue.

Besides the skill set and emotional support I needed to get here, I am so grateful for the people I've met in my blogging and publishing journey. I'm happy to have my agent, Kate, by my side, always supportive and honest. Thanks to my photographer friends, Becky and Linnea, for their help with some of the daunting steps of sharing my work visually, and thanks to my network of supportive Portland Bloggers friends for sharing this excitement with me and always being available by email! Thank you!

# Preface

I've been sewing for as long as I can remember. I'm lucky to have grown up with many chances to learn how things work and try my hand at everything from stripping the baseboards and doors of our historic home to making my own Barbie clothes.

During college I started to sew more for myself, and I got more experimental. Some of the new approaches worked and others didn't, but I learned from both the successes and the mistakes. Now I use many of the basic techniques I first learned from my mom alongside the tricks I developed on my own.

In 2009 I began my blog, *Adventures in Dressmaking*. Out of grad school and underemployed, I found myself sewing and creating home decor and furniture makeovers with my "idle" time. A friend suggested I keep track of all my projects in a blog, and the rest is history!

The blog has grown to reach a dedicated community of inspired and inspiring DIYers who are enthusiastic about sewing, fashion, and decor. (The blog is now called *Create/Enjoy*.) I've shared many tutorials for ways I remade a specific type of sweater or imitated a particular seasonal trend (such as my early J. Crew–inspired appliqué tees and my ever-versatile cuffed cutoff shorts). I often get questions from readers and friends about how to re-create a favorite style from a movie or remake an old dress with great fabric into something trendy again.

I also get questions about more basic essential clothing fixes and refashioning advice. I find myself sharing the same tips and techniques quite often.

That's a big part of the reason why I wrote this book. Read on to find sewing tutorials and projects that are the all-time most requested by my readers and friends, as well as all the tried-and-true tricks I use every day to make something perfect out of something plain. I want to give you the skills to solve the most universal clothing makeover needs, plus some ideas and strategies to get you thinking creatively about your own refashioning transformations. This book will provide the foundation you need to make your wardrobe work for you. I hope it will be a favorite resource of yours as you hone your skills to spend less and look better!

# Why DIY?

How many times have you bought something in a store and only worn it once? Maybe you realized it didn't look that great after all; maybe you got tired of the style; maybe you changed size and it didn't fit anymore. I've had all of those problems and more. Mass-produced clothes often don't have the most flattering fit or most lasting quality, and it's hard to predict how you'll look or want to dress in a year or two. If you don't have the tools and skills to alter your clothes, you're stuck with exactly what you buy.

Enter *DIY Wardrobe Makeovers*! This book is a primer on altering, remaking, and maximizing your clothing to work better for you. Whether your closet is hiding jeans that are too long, a dated button-down shirt that's no longer flattering, or a slightly stretched-out sweater in a great color, you'll find an easy DIY wardrobe fix for the most common clothing problems. In this book, I share some key step-by-step techniques to improve, revive, and rescue your clothing. Your made-over garments will not only fit better but will also showcase your amazing sense of style.

> If you don't have the tools and skills to alter your clothes, you're stuck with exactly what you buy.

DIY projects are empowering! The DIY trend is a growing movement, and it is no wonder. Learning to make, or remake, things at home gives you the confidence—and self-sufficiency—to create whatever you need or desire.

Saving money is usually a good thing, as are conserving resources and reducing waste. Restyling your wardrobe will allow you to shop your closet instead of relegating ill-fitting or dated fashions to the thrift store while continually buying more new clothes.

Style is all about self-expression. Set your own trends by adding a unique touch to what you wear and show off clothes and looks that you love.

As a lifelong sewist, a bargain hunter, and a pro thrift-store shopper, it's become second nature to me to make or repair my own clothing when I want a new style or better fit. I'm proud to admit that I've brought home treasures from the thrift store and scoured clearance and sale racks for things that I can rescue or modify with simple, small adjustments—adding a piece of lace, bringing up the hem, or tweaking a neckline—and made them perfect for me. Buying from thrift stores, remaking old pieces from my closet, or finding new-to-me pieces at clothing swaps with friends, in particular, make me feel better about my consumer impact on the planet, about avoiding the social costs involved in the clothing industry, and of course, about saving money!

After perfecting the flared-dress-pants-into-skinny-cropped-pants transformation, I learned long ago that I don't need to spend much to get trendy things when I can make them myself out of what I already own or can purchase at less expensive prices. I find inspiration everywhere, and I always look at how things are constructed to figure out if I can make something similar myself. The DIY mind-set has rewired my brain. And now, it's almost easier and less stressful to DIY a flattering piece of clothing that I like instead of spending big bucks on a store version that might not be quite right anyway.

Why should you learn to do it yourself, you ask? There are tons of reasons!

**Trendiness //** One great thing about knowing how to make your own clothes and accessories is the ability to update your look quickly and follow trends with what you already own. Get the look you want now, within your budget, and tailored to fit you exactly. It is simple to refashion a basic into something that feels au courant.

**Cost //** When done right, DIY fashion can be significantly cheaper than buying store-bought, and you can often get a very similar look to a specific piece you've been eyeing. It's easy and low cost to get a custom fit and style.

**Creativity //** DIY does not mean simply copying others' ideas—it is about expressing yourself. A huge part of the DIY attitude is thinking off the hanger and creating unique items that show your individuality. This book will also get you ready to add personality and fashionable flair to tired or boring pieces.

# Getting Inspired

Before you begin to create or remake, you need an idea. I always feel inspired after watching a beautiful movie that evokes a theme or fashion moment or after window shopping at the mall and looking at what's new. Sometimes it helps to get some new perspective. When you want to find ideas for clothing makeover projects and pieces you want to try making for yourself, check out these resources:

**Magazines**   Any kind of magazine, either for fashion, health, beauty, or home decor, can provide plenty of inspiration. I love looking at blogs and celebrity street style images for current trends, and I have several style idols whom I enjoy following for hot new looks to try.

**Pinterest**   Pinterest can be overwhelming, but if you use it strategically you can identify some great ideas and conveniently save them to your own pinboards for fashion or DIYing. If you find a Pinterest user whose style you like, search through her boards for images, and then check out the original sources for them and any other boards they were pinned to. I use Pinterest as a catalog of images to search through—if I want to use a piece of fake fur, I might search "cute fake fur" or "fur style" and see what pops up. I also enjoy looking back through my pinboards to remind myself of recent faves.

**TV and movies**   If you've ever seen a movie and just wanted to be *in* it, you'll know what I mean about getting instantly inspired. For example, I love watching movies from or about the 70s or 80s—they always make me want to wear my hair a certain way, or add a particular color to my wardrobe, or find an accessory like a great long necklace or shoulder bag that reminds me of the music, lighting, and mood of the movie. Sometimes you may see a piece you want to copy exactly, but often it's just about capturing the feel of a great story or place.

**Favorite stores or catalogs** // Sometimes catalogs, ads, and store displays speak to our personal sense of style, as well as reinforce a brand's image. While we're all far more creative and individual than the store mannequins displaying a particular brand, it sometimes helps to have a store's or designer's line in mind when you're shopping for fabric or sketching a design. Look at your favorite fabrics, colors, textures, shapes, and accessories, and how things are layered and put together.

# Learning about Clothes

Once you're inspired to DIY or have an item that needs alteration, you'll also want to get a better understanding of your clothes. Along with trial and error and learning by doing, there are a few more ways you can build up your knowledge.

**Look inside your clothes** // Examine five of your woven button-down shirts, for example, and see what they have in common. They probably have small serged seam allowances inside, maybe some with topstitching, although the nicer ones have smooth French seams or a lining hiding all the seams. Your shirts may have small hems on the bottom and cuffs with one or two rows of topstitching. They could have center back yokes with double layers of fabric—the inside is a partial lining, used to reinforce the fabric and tag, and hide raw edges. Look at how things are made, and then if you ever cut them apart or make your own, you'll have an image of what they're supposed to look like finished. Take pictures. Check out your jeans next, or your skirts. Have a good look around at the insides and edges.

**Go fabric shopping** // Head to a fabric store and see what is available. Usually fabrics are sorted by use and type, often with seasonal apparel fabrics up front. There are also sections for basics such as denim, corduroy, shirtings (for dress shirts or blouses), flannel, fleece, and more. Think about what the clothes in your wardrobe are made of. There's a reason pants are often made with heavier fabrics such as twills but tops can be made using lightweight polyester, cotton, or linen. The fabrics you choose will determine how the garment wears and drapes. I recommend specific types of fabrics for the projects in this book, but going to fabric stores will help you recognize what you need for anything in your wardrobe.

**Try on your least favorite clothes** // Well, maybe not your least favorite, but check out the pieces in your closet that don't quite work and identify why. Do you rarely wear those khakis because they're a little too short? Is that sweater too big in the waist, so you only feel good wearing it with a belt? That shrunken tee in the color you love—maybe you can keep what you like about it but turn it into something new—maybe a comfy dress with a contrasting skirt?

Then you can get started with this book! Sort the pieces into a few piles and see what you've got. This will help you pick a first project or skill to get started with in this book! I'm sure many of you have a pair of jeans that you'd wear a lot more often if the back waistband fit a little better, or a blouse you'd layer more if it didn't have sleeves. After you pull out the garments from your wardrobe that could use a little work, you can match them up with some of the techniques or projects in this book and make them into something new!

# More Remaking Ideas

As you can probably tell, there are almost endless possibilities for refashioning and remaking your clothes. Once you've mastered the ones in this book, get creative! Below are a few more of my favorite wardrobe fixes and remakes to try.

Turn a dress into a skirt by cutting off the bodice and giving it a new waistband (elastic or structured like the one in Blouse-into-Dress Makeover, page 129).

Cover stains with fabric or trim embellishments (see (Nearly) Unlimited Embellishment Ideas, page 157).

Add straps to a strapless dress using coordinating fabric.

Cut off the sleeves of a dress and finish the armholes with bias binding, as in Silky Blouse Makeover (page 118) or Tie-Waist Blouse Makeover (page 122).

Add a Peter Pan collar to a plain sweater or tee.

Instead of classic denim cut-offs, make cut-offs from colored jeans or khakis. You can even give them a nice hem for a dressier look.

# When Not to Refashion

Unfortunately, no matter how skilled a sewist you become, there may be times when you can't make a piece of clothing work indefinitely.

Some clothes simply cannot be made bigger. Often there are ways to make an old favorite item slightly larger, longer, or looser in one place, but some items just don't have enough extra fabric to allow this. They would be better transformed into home decor projects, children's clothing or small accessories, or simply given away.

Some fabrics get so worn, they are beyond repair or no longer worth salvaging. I've seen silk or silk-blend blouses fall apart with washing and aging; some rips and stretching are irreparable. Even if the color and fit are still good, it may not be possible to mend the holes smoothly.

Vintage clothes can have the potential to be antique or valuable in their own right, and you don't necessarily want to turn them into something else.

# Great Moments in Clothing Makeover History

Now that I've been making and remaking my clothes for quite a few years, I've collected favorite projects and memorable moments when DIYing was really the greatest solution to a clothing or style problem. But you may not have experienced that thrill yet, so let me share with you (or remind you of) a few great moments you may remember (or want to watch!) in movies and TV:

- The part in *The Sound of Music* when Maria turns old curtains into play clothes for the children has always been one of my favorites. She doesn't want the perfectly good fabric to go to waste, and she wants the children to have some more relaxed clothing—what a perfect solution! Totally something I would do, although I can't imagine how she had time to make all those outfits so fast!

- When I saw the movie *Pretty in Pink* when I was a teenager, it was far after the era that Molly Ringwald's pink, high-necked, puff-sleeved prom dress might have looked fashionable, and I have to admit my best friend and I were baffled by the strange silhouette she created out of an older prom dress. But it's the thought that counts with DIY experimenting, and I did always admire the character's resourcefulness. She makes her friend's old prom dress truly her own when she remakes it into a new style.

- I always thought it was pretty cool that the main character of *The Gilmore Girls*, the mother, Lorelai, knew how to sew. In one episode she talks about how she made a baby jumper for Rory out one of her old concert T-shirts. What a cool idea, for saving money and sharing your style with a trendy little kid.

- It's not super realistic or happy and inspiring, but the dramatic scene in Tim Burton's 1992 *Batman* totally shows the power of taking control of your clothing and remaking something old into something that fits your new look. What a transformation when Michelle Pfeiffer remakes a black vinyl trench coat into the sleek Catwoman jumpsuit, using a vintage sewing machine, no less. I hope we can remake our old pieces with less emotional turmoil!

- *Gone with the Wind*—while most of the costumes are pretty over-the-top and unrealistic, it is true to life that ladies in the 1860s sometimes made over their old dresses to follow the changing fashions, as Scarlett O'Hara does with her white-flounced summer ball gown, which she turns into a bustle dress many years later.

- The sweet scene in the Disney cartoon of *Cinderella* shows quite a few steps of how the mice and birds remake Cinderella's mother's old ball gown by adding trimmings and an overskirt to match a picture in a fashion book. Measuring, counting lace yardage, threading a needle... "We can do it, we can do it," sing the mice, inspiring children for decades to learn to sew!

# How This Book Will Help You DIY

Of course, you don't have to start out by making yourself a complete wardrobe from yards of curtain fabric. That kind of project probably seems a little intimidating to you (or even to an accomplished sewist). Turning an old nightgown into a fashionable top may also seem intimidating, or unnecessary. While many of us now have the sewing skills and experience to design and create clothing from scratch or from challenging materials, we didn't always have those skills.

If you're less experienced, a great way to learn to make your own clothes is by working with pieces you already have in your closet. Sure, you can go buy a muumuu or funky men's dress shirt at a thrift shop and play around with it, but why not start with refashioning and altering the wardrobe you already own? Maybe, after trying the projects in this book, you'll love your sewing machine so much you'll want to start doing more complex projects and making new things every season. Maybe you'll start studying must-have clothing in the stores or magazines, so you can re-create them yourself. Fashions change with time, but the step-by-step techniques and DIY style projects in this book will give you the know-how you need to keep refashioning for years to come.

If you're new to sewing clothes, you may want to start with Infinity Scarf Makeover (page 78) or Colorblock Sweater Makeover (page 84) to get your feet wet. Other satisfying projects for beginners are Contrast-Sleeve Tee (page 89) and Flared Pants to Skinny Pants (page 110).

# About the Instructions

There are no paper sewing patterns included in this book. For custom-fit alterations and refashioned projects, you won't need them. The instructions in most of these projects assume you're starting with a garment that is in a recognizable shape and size—while you could turn a trench coat into a newsboy cap if you wanted to, the most common DIY clothing makeover projects I find myself doing are simpler ones.

Most of these projects will work best for those in the average adult size range of XS–XL, but with the right materials, you can easily modify them for children or plus-size wearers. We'll talk about measuring yourself to ensure you're getting the right fit. If you're starting with clothes that are close to your size, you should have no problem doing these projects.

Each tutorial and project is illustrated with step-by-step photos that show you every part of the process and how to work with the typical inner construction of each type of garment. At the beginning of each project, you'll find a list of the tools you need as well as a list of materials and my recommendations for the type of fabric or garment to start with. After you get the hang of working with the most popular, easiest materials, you can certainly explore other choices and see what comes of them.

The alteration technique tutorials are categorized by technique: *Take It In, Take It Up, Let It Out,* and *Let It Down.* These simple fixes are great ways for you to begin taking control of your wardrobe. Plus, getting comfortable with basics such as hemming

pants or adding a facing to make a skirt longer will be very helpful for opening your mind to the more creative possibilities suggested in the DIY style projects. The possibilities are endless, and after you master some basic techniques, all of them will be within reach.

The DIY style projects generally fall into three categories:

**Refashions,** in which a garment is transformed into another type of garment, such as a shirt into a skirt;

**Remakes,** in which an item is customized and made more personal, fashionable, and flattering; and

**Embellishing,** in which a piece gets a little stylish flair to decorate it. The easiest and simplest projects are listed first within each group.

## Note

Metric conversions are included throughout this book for the convenience of anyone who uses metric measurements.

# Basic Tools

Before you dive into making over your wardrobe, you'll need to have some basic tools and materials.

Photo by Nakalan McKay

# Tools and Materials

Rescuing and DIYing your clothing does require a few sewing tools. You may already have some of these, and the others are worth the small initial investment. Your sewing tools will last a long time if you keep them dedicated to this purpose, and your projects will turn out better if you use the appropriate materials.

## SEWING MACHINE

I use a sewing machine for most of my clothing projects because it is fast and easy, and it creates lasting seams. You don't have to have one for all of the projects in this book, but you'll probably want to get or borrow one to make most of them. The instructions assume you are using one.

You don't need a top-of-the-line model, but the cheapest ones are made from a lot of plastic parts and may break more quickly and be frustrating. There are many good used machines out there. Many older machines are made from high-quality metal parts, so they keep their alignment and don't break easily.

**If you are buying a machine, look for these key features:**

**Free arm with a removable extension table** // Necessary for working on pant legs and armholes.

**Zipper foot** // Zippers are often the first thing to break on a favorite dress or skirt. You can replace them easily with a new zipper and this special foot for your machine. Most machines come with a zipper foot, but if yours doesn't you can buy one separately.

**Built-in blind hem stitch** // You can hem a skirt, dress, sleeve, or anything with a straight stitch, but this variation on a zigzag stitch makes a beautiful, professional seam that is less visible on the right side of the fabric.

**One-step buttonhole** // Trust me, the multi-step ones are a pain! With a one-step buttonhole feature, all you need to make perfect buttonholes is a steady hand, good thread, and the right tension settings for your fabric.

Basic sewing machine with removable extension table

Sewing machine with extension table removed

# CUTTING TOOLS

**Sharp, tiny scissors or snips** // You never know when you'll need a pair of these to open up a seam, snip off a button, or clip a seam allowance. The precision you can get with small scissors or snips is essential for modifying your clothes without hacking and cutting too far or too much. I recommend you get a pair of tiny scissors with pointed ends so that you can use one side to go under a stitch if you need to, or if you don't have a seam ripper handy. Scissors with rounded edges will also work. Just make sure your little scissors are sharp enough to cut thread and bits of fabric without any resistance. **A**

**Fabric scissors** // For cutting more than a few inches of fabric, particularly lightweight or finer fabric, you'll need sharp scissors that cut cleanly and don't pull or snag the weave. Get a good pair of strong sewing scissors, and don't ever use them for paper or anything else—it will dull them, making it harder to cut fabric. **B**

**Pinking shears** // These old fashioned–sounding scissors are great for keeping edges from raveling. Use them on seam allowances after you sew but before you press, or for a decorative effect. **C**

**Seam ripper** // These sharp little picks are extremely helpful when taking out a machine-sewn seam, something you'll often do before modifying a garment (and during your project if you make a mistake). The pointed end slips under the stitch on one side of the fabric, and the curved blade part cuts the thread (for more info, see Removing Stitches, page 35). **D**

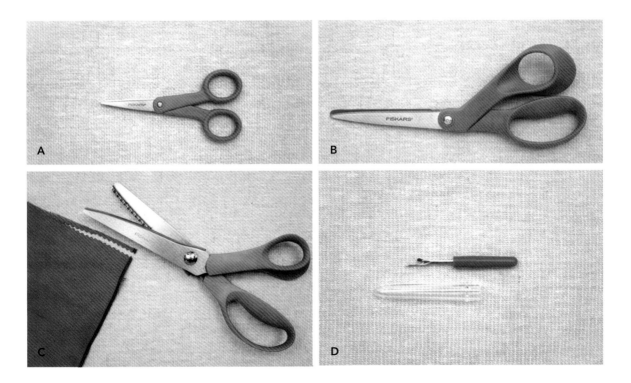

# NEEDLES, THREAD, AND PINS

**Sewing machine needles** // Standard needles have a "universal" point; however, other needle points are available in common sizes for some specific fabrics like knits, denim, and leather. Choose a needle size based on the weight of your fabric. Use a size 60/8 needle for lightweight or sheer fabrics, a 70/10 or 80/12 (the most common size I use) for medium-weight fabric, and a 90/14 or 100/16 for heavy fabrics like denim or canvas.

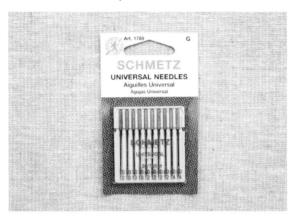

I also suggest getting a twin needle, with two needles coming from a single base that you insert into your machine. These are great for hemming knit garments—they keep the raw edge from rolling on the inside and they mimic a store-bought

garment finish. Twin needles come in different needle sizes and spacing widths, and you can use them on any machine that can do a zigzag (as long as the width of the needles can fit through the hole in your presser foot and throat plate). Use a straight stitch with a twin needle, but sew from the right side of the garment (as shown in Hemming, Method 3, page 40).

**Hand sewing needles** // Hand sewing needles come in many varieties; you'll want what's called a "sharp." These have a sharp point and medium length when compared with other specialized types. They come in several sizes (which are not completely standard across all companies) ranging from size 1 (the longest and thickest) to size 10 or 12 (the shortest and thinnest). I typically use about a 6 or 8.

You'll also want tapestry needles for sweaters and loosely woven things. They are thicker and longer, and have a blunt point and large eye so you can use embroidery floss or yarn in them. I prefer a large tapestry needle, about a size 13, for sweaters and other mending projects, such as darning a hole or attaching a hook and eye on a knit garment.

**All-purpose thread in your favorite colors** // While you can use any color in a pinch, one key to making your sewing look indistinguishable from a quality store-bought piece is matching the thread color to the garment. White or bright thread will contrast with a dark color, or vice versa, and will stick out like a sore thumb.

You can buy small sampler packs of threads while you build your thread collection. I usually buy Gütermann basic polyester, but sometimes I use an all-cotton thread for topstitching. (Cotton is not as strong as polyester, and it can accumulate fuzz when used in a sewing machine.)

When using a sewing machine, use matching or close-in-color thread in the bobbin—sometimes it's the bobbin side of the seam that shows on the outside. Wind a full bobbin in your project color before you start so you can complete the sewing without having to stop and wind a new bobbin.

**Tip** You may come across big, inexpensive collections of thread at thrift stores or by combing a relative's unused supply. If you do find a stash of old thread, test it out before you use it. Old thread can sometimes be weak and break easily. If it's still usable, this is a great way to get thread in a new range of colors!

**Straight pins** // Pinning before you sew can make all the difference between a misaligned, crooked, or puckered seam and a flat, beautiful line. Pins hold pieces in place when sewing. If you're using a machine, in a pinch you can sew over pins that are placed perpendicular to the seam, but they can break or dull your machine's needle (or worse), so take them out right before the needle reaches them if you can.

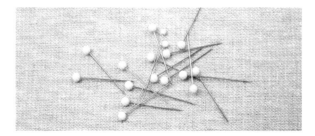

**Pincushion** // Everyone has a preference on how to store pins. I like using a magnetic pincushion or holder. With one of these, you don't have to put your pins back with absolute precision; the magnet will just grab them. Also, pins won't fall off when the cushion is knocked over. A simple round fabric pincushion works, too, but it doesn't hold as many pins as a magnetic pincushion does, and you have to be a little more careful putting pins back into it.

**Tip** It's good to have a fabric marking tool or two at hand. A disappearing-ink fabric pen, or a piece of tailor's chalk for dark fabric, is extremely helpful for marking on a garment where you need to make changes. I use a marking tool when pins might fall out, such as on very lightweight or stretchy fabric, and when marking button or buttonhole placement.

## MEASURING TOOLS

**Measuring tape** // You'll need to be able to measure yourself or whomever you're sewing for with a flexible sewing measuring tape.

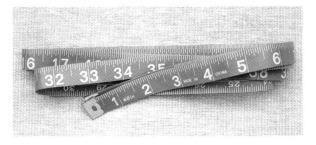

**Quilting ruler** // I use my large, clear quilting ruler as a straightedge as well as a measuring guide when cutting.

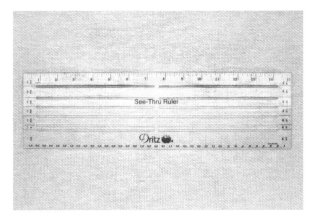

**Hem gauge** // I recommend you get a hem gauge, which often doubles as a point turner too. This is typically a short metal ruler with a movable guide that helps you make an even hem. The plastic ones are sturdier for point-turning but don't have a movable marker.

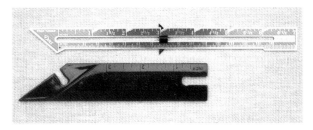

## PRESSING TOOLS

**Iron** // Just like matching your thread or pinning to keep your fabric aligned, properly pressing your garment can make all the difference between something you're not proud of and something you love. At each step of the sewing process, it's important to press your seams (often flat to one side) so the fabric looks smooth on the outside. Some fabrics can take more heat than others, so make sure you use the correct setting on your iron (see Pressing, page 41). You can easily find a cheap iron online or at a discount store, but the more expensive models usually provide more heat, so if you work on many heavy cottons or linens, you may want a pricier model.

**Ironing board** // Along with your iron you'll probably need an ironing board (large or small), although a towel folded in half on a floor or table will work in a serious pinch.

**Spray bottle** // A spray bottle for water is good to have when pressing, for those really tricky wrinkles or heavy fabric.

## FABRICS AND NOTIONS

**Assorted fabrics, elastics, and other embellishments** // While all the projects in this book begin with ready-made garments, some project ideas can use additional materials such as fabric or lace yardage to complete the refashion. Each project will specify the additional materials you need, and all of them can be found at a local fabric store or online (see Resources, page 159).

You can also reuse part of another garment or fabric from a thrift store instead of new materials, as long as the fabric is an appropriate type. I'll give tips about the fabric weight and fiber content to use in each project. When you use new fabric of natural fiber content, make sure to prewash it according to the care instructions so the finished garment doesn't shrink when you wash it later.

I prefer to sew on natural fibers (cotton, linen, wool, and silk) rather than polyester or synthetic fibers, and they're nicer to wear, too. The weight, weave, and texture of the fabric also make a big difference. Slippery, shiny, or sheer fabrics are typically more difficult to sew on, or at least require more patience. Knit fabrics require a special (ball point) machine needle and a zigzag stitch so the thread can stretch with the fabric. Once you get the hang of sewing them, knits can be very forgiving.

Woven cotton fabrics such as a corduroy, twill, or shirting are generally the easiest to sew on, though they wouldn't work for some of the DIY projects, so make note of the tips and recommendations before buying fabric.

The projects at the end of the book, in the section (Nearly) Unlimited Embellishment Ideas (page 157), are great for using fun trims, braids, and ribbons that catch your eye at the fabric store or online. As you learn to refashion your clothes, you may find yourself shopping for additional notions such as buttons and decorative elastics, too.

## Standard Sewing Supplies

For each tutorial or project, you'll need some of these items in addition to any special tools or materials listed.

- Sewing machine
- Thread snips
- Fabric scissors
- Seam ripper
- Thread in matching colors
- Straight pins and pincushion
- Measuring tape and/or clear ruler
- Hem gauge
- Iron

Photo by Nakalan McKay

# Terminology

## Fabric Terms

**Bias** // The bias grain of the fabric is the diagonal angle you find when you fold the fabric into a right triangle. Bias-cut edges are very stretchy. A dress cut on the bias drapes over every curve, and narrow strips of fabric cut on the bias will stretch around armholes or a neck edge. Bias tape, a strip of fabric 1″ to 2″ (2.5–5cm) wide cut on the bias grain, is very useful for covering the edges and curves of a project. You can buy premade bias tape or make your own.

**Centers** // On garments, the "centers" are the centers of the front and back of the top and/or bottom, depending on what you're making. Symmetry is important in sewing, because you attach fronts to backs, tops to bottoms, and sides to sides. Everything needs to line up and be sewn together at the right place. The center front of a dress bodice needs to line up perfectly with the center front of the skirt or waistband, so it doesn't look crooked or skewed.

Whenever I make anything, I fold the fabric in half the long way (along the lengthwise grain and selvage) and clip a *tiny* triangle at the fold of each piece, on the top and bottom edges. That way, when I put pieces together, I can match my notches and keep everything centered. The notch (the clipped-out triangle) is hidden in the seam allowance and never shows. When these instructions say "find your centers," fold the pieces in half before you start sewing and place a mark, pin, or notch at the center front and back, and sides if applicable, so you know the pieces will line up with each other when you pin them together.

This chapter presents a list of key terms you'll encounter throughout this book and on any of your future sewing adventures.

**Dart** // A dart is a sewn-in fold in the fabric, used to make a garment three-dimensional to curve to the body. Some of the simplest darts are small triangles that taper from the waist of a skirt or bodice to the bust or hip line. Adding darts at the waist of a boxy or baggy garment will give it shape.

**Grain** // Grain refers to the weave of the fabric. The lengthwise grain (warp) of the fabric runs parallel to the selvage and is the strongest grain of the fabric. Cut out garments with the lengthwise grain running from top to bottom of the item. Think of the selvage edges as making up the side seams or center back seams. The crosswise grain (weft) of the fabric runs from selvage to selvage and measures the width of the fabric. Think of it as the width of your garments, so cut waistbands or other bands with some give on the crosswise grain.

**Raw edge** // This is the cut or torn edge of the fabric, as opposed to the clean selvage edge or an edge that's finished with serger stitches, zigzag stitches, pinking cuts, or a bias fabric binding. Depending on the fabric and stitch you use, raw edges can unravel, make a seam weaker, or leave little pieces of thread and fluff all over your workspace. Store-bought clothes don't usually have exposed raw edges in them, and homemade clothing or improvements will last longer if you finish any raw edges as you put the garment together. If the inside of a garment is going to be exposed or rubbed at all when worn, and if it's not on the selvage as in the sides of straight skirt panels, I often zigzag the seam allowances closed to keep all the raw edges in place and keep the fabric from unraveling.

**Seam allowance** // The extra fabric between the seam stitching and the fabric edge, often ½″ (13mm) on commercially made garments, is the seam allowance. This width of fabric keeps the seams from pulling out. Seam allowances are added to finished garment measurements when you cut out the pieces. On tailored clothing, there is often up to 1″ (2.5cm) of seam allowance; if a garment becomes too tight, tailors can often let it out by ½″ (13mm), which can make a big difference in fit. On T-shirts and other knits made with industrial sergers, there is often virtually no seam allowance—the seam allowance is less than ¼″ (6mm) and is finished with stitching, so it is difficult to let these out. Homemade clothes usually have ½″ to ⅝″ (13mm–1.5cm) seam allowances. The throat plate of your machine will probably have vertical lines at these measurements that you can use as guides to line up your fabric while you sew. It's very important to use the same seam allowance for the entire length of each seam, because if you wobble while sewing it may show on the outside and the fabric may pucker.

**Selvage** // The selvage is the manufactured finished edge of fabric, usually a slightly different color or weave than the rest of the fabric. On quilting and home decorating fabrics, the selvage may be printed with the brand or name of the fabric. The selvage runs the whole length on both side edges of the fabric. Some sewists cut off the selvage because it can shrink at a different rate than the rest of the fabric. But because the selvage is the strongest part of the fabric, I like to use it for straight edges of garments, such as the center back of a dress or the side seams of a gathered or loose skirt.

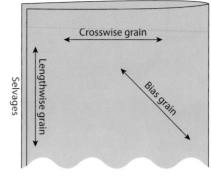

Cut or torn edge
Crosswise grain
Lengthwise grain
Selvages
Bias grain

# Sewing Machine Terms

**Feed dogs** // The feed teeth or dogs are the rows of pointed metal teeth under the presser foot. They control how fast the fabric moves along the seam and therefore how long the stitches are. They also help you sew straight. Make sure the feed dogs are up when you sew—freehand or free-motion sewing and quilting sometimes require putting them down, but you'll need their guidance when sewing these projects.

**Presser foot** // The presser foot is the metal piece that holds the fabric in place while you sew. Newer machines won't sew if the foot isn't down, but on older machines, make sure you lower that foot—you'll create a loopy mess of thread under the seam and have to take it out if you don't. For most of the sewing in this book, you'll use a basic presser foot, but switch to a zipper foot if you're inserting a zipper, or a walking foot if you're sewing on a knit.

**Tension** // Sewing machine stitches are controlled by two tension settings: The top thread tension and the bobbin thread tension. If either setting is adjusted incorrectly for the fabric and/or thread you're using, the quality of the stitches will be poor and the seams will be weak. Both tensions are usually easy to adjust. The top tension is typically adjusted using a knob or dial on the front or side of the machine. The bobbin tension is adjusted by turning a screw on the bobbin case. Consult your machine manual to find out exactly where the tensions are adjusted.

If you see the bobbin thread on the top fabric you are sewing, the top tension is too tight and/or the bottom tension is too loose.

If you can see the top thread on the underside of what you are sewing, the top tension is too loose and/or the bobbin tension is too tight.

Before you start a project, it's a good idea to sew a bit on a test piece of fabric of the same weight as the fabric you'll be sewing with and take a good look at the stitching. If the tension isn't right, adjust the top tension first, then try adjusting the bobbin tension.

**Throat plate** // The throat plate covers the bobbin mechanism and usually has seam guides that you can use to make sure you are sewing straight and with a consistent seam allowance. Most machines' throat plates show notches for ½″ (13mm) and ⅝″ (17mm), the seam allowances I use most often for garment sewing. It has openings for the feed dogs and for the needle and thread.

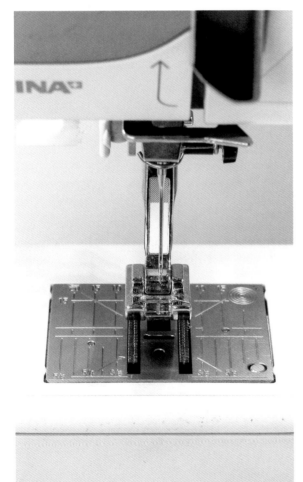

# Stitches

**Backstitch** // When using a sewing machine, use about two backstitches at the beginning and end of a seam to anchor stitches instead of tying knots. Rather than beginning a seam with the needle at the edge of the fabric, move the needle into the seam. Sew in reverse for a few stitches, and then sew the seam. At the end of the seam, sew a few more stitches in reverse.

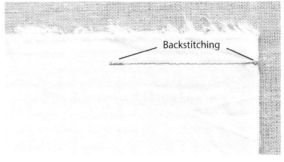

Backstitching

**Basting** // Basting stitches are large (about 5mm / 5 stitches per inch), loose, often temporary stitches that hold the fabric together like super pins. If you have slippery or tricky fabric or multiple layers to sew together, you may want to baste the layers together in a stitch that's easy to pull out if you need to. Instead of backstitching a basting seam, leave the thread tails long so the seam can be more easily removed. You can also use basting stitches to hold pleats in place before attaching them to a waistband.

**Blind hem stitch** // Using a machine blind hem stitch is a good alternative to hand stitching a hem. This stitch can be a little confusing and tricky, so practice on some scrap fabric first. By folding the main fabric back on itself next to the inside top edge of the hem, you can use this stitch to grab a few fibers of the outer fabric, keeping the hem in place almost invisibly. Nicer dress pants and dresses will have this stitch on the hems. Some machines allow you to adjust the width as well as the length of the stitch. My machine has a special blind hem foot to guide me as I sew.

**Stitch in-the-ditch** // This kind of seam is nearly invisible on the outside if you do it right—it takes a lot of careful concentration, but it is key for finishing the waistbands of pants and skirts, and it is also used for cuffs. You'll see it in between the waistband and main fabric of many pairs of pants, for example—it's a straight row of stitches that goes through the top fabric and the back facing of the band and is only visible up close. Make sure you use thread that very closely matches your outer fabric.

**Gathering** // Gathering stitches are similar to basting stitches in that they are also long and sewn with a loose machine tension, but after the seam is sewn, the top thread is pulled tight to bring the fabric together. Gathering stitches don't show when the garment is done, so use whatever thread color you want and leave the ends very long on both sides—and don't backstitch on either end. You'll pull on the top thread to tighten the fabric up on itself and create a nice puff on the other side. Gathering is commonly used for skirts and sleeves. On heavy or unruly fabric, use two parallel rows of long stitches to gather and pull on both top threads at once.

**Straight stitch** // On a machine, this is usually stitch number 0 or 1, and it's the most common stitch you'll use. By hand, it's a running stitch or half-backstitch. Either way, it's a straight line of sewing that you'll use for most seams. On a machine, I recommend a medium-length stitch (2.5–3mm / 10–12 stitches per inch) unless it's a seam that will bear a lot of strain or weight, in which case a smaller stitch will be safer.

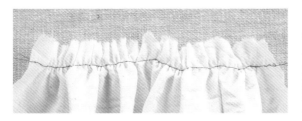

**Serging** // Sergers are a special type of sewing machine that sews a seam and finishs the edges at the same time, often trimming the excess seam allowance in the process. Most commercially made clothing is finished with serged seams and edges. You don't need a serger for the projects in this book, but if you have one it will allow you to make professionally finished seams.

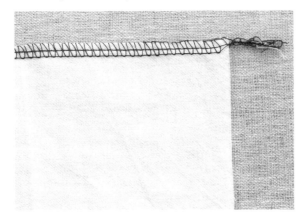

**Top stitch** // Topstitching is visible, often decorative stitching. There's topstitching on most jeans inseams and pockets in thick yellow thread, and on blouse cuff and collar edges. Use a stitch length that matches or looks nice on the fabric you are using because the stitches show and can be a decorative element. Topstitching keeps fabric in its pressed-back position and is useful for keeping seam allowances or the underside of a garment lying flat.

**Zigzag** // Zigzag stitches are very useful if you don't have a serger to finish raw edges and for sewing straight seams on knits. I often recommend zigzagging the edge of a seam allowance (with a short, wide zigzag) to keep the threads from unraveling on the inside. When you sew on knits, use a very long, relatively narrow zigzag stitch (try 4–5mm / 5–6 stitches per inch long and 2–3mm wide) for all the long seams instead of a straight stitch because knit fabric stretches but woven thread seams don't, unless you give them the width of a zigzag to pull out and in a little bit.

# Sewing Skills

This chapter includes descriptions of some basic skills and steps. Use it as a handy reference guide when working on projects.

Photo by Nakalan McKay

# Using Your Sewing Machine

The majority of the projects in this book are written assuming you will be using a sewing machine. Don't worry! Even if you're an absolute beginner, most simple sewing machines are easy and straightforward to operate. A quick demonstration by a friend who sews can be really helpful. It's also a good idea to read over your sewing machine manual.

## Here's a primer on what you need to know to operate a sewing machine:

**Threading the machine** // If you're new to sewing or are using an unfamiliar machine, check the manual for the correct threading path. Make sure the top thread and bobbin thread are the right color and type for your project, and don't skip any of the hooks or thread catches. Use a "universal" needle unless a specialized one is called for, and match the needle size to the type of fabric as detailed under Sewing Machine Needles (page 19).

**Loading/winding bobbins** // All machines include a mechanism for winding thread from a spool onto a bobbin. Follow the machine's instructions and load the bobbin exactly as instructed to ensure the right tension. If you're using a machine you've used before, you may already have several bobbins loaded with different thread colors. If the machine and equipment are new to you, you may have to load a new bobbin each time you start a project of a different color. Use a matching thread color to make your sewing look professional.

**Starting and ending a seam** // There is no need to tie any knots when machine sewing; the backstitch feature of the machine will do it for you (see Backstitch, page 27).

**Tip** It's tempting to just grab a bobbin that's already loaded with thread when you're anxious to get started on a project. But if you don't have one that's close in color to the top thread you're using, it's definitely worth the extra few moments to load a matching bobbin. I don't fill mine all the way if I know I won't be sewing with a color for more than a few seams.

**Setting the right stitch** // There are a lot of variables when it comes to machine stitches—length, width, type, and even the tension between the top and bottom threads. Each project specifies the purpose of the seams you need to make. Refer to Straight Stitch (page 28), Zigzag (page 29), and Tension (page 26) for recommended settings. Generally, thinner fabrics require a lower tension since they move along more easily on the machine's feed dogs, and heavier fabrics require higher tension settings to pull the bobbin thread up through the layers. It's always a good idea to test out stitch settings on a scrap piece of fabric before starting on the real thing.

When trying a new stitch or a new type of fabric, practice with scrap fabric and see what happens before you start working on a project.

# Hand Finishing

Even when sewing clothes by machine, the last few steps often require some good, old-fashioned hand sewing. Here are a few of the most common techniques you'll use when sewing by hand.

**Threading the needle** // It's a simple step, but remember to use a single strand of thread when you don't want stitches to show— as with hems or when attaching trims. Use two strands of thread when sewing something that will bear any strain or weight, such as buttons or other fasteners. To double up thread, cut a strand twice as long as you want, push one end through the needle, double the thread back on itself so that the two ends meet, and tie an overhand knot, treating the two strands as one.

**Sewing on a button** // This is an essential skill, but not everyone knows how to do it quickly and well.

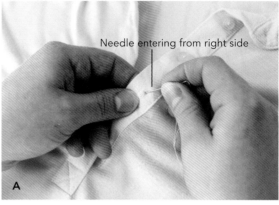

Needle entering from right side

**A**

**B**

**C**

**D**

**1.** Unwind a thread strand to about 18″ (45.5cm). Insert one end of the thread into the needle's eye. Double the thread back on itself until the ends meet and the needle falls in the center, and tie a knot.

**2.** Next, determine where to place the button. If it just popped off, you may be able to use the old thread holes as a guide. If there are none, button the rest of the placket or align the left and right sides, and put a pin through the buttonhole to find the location on the underlapped placket where the button should be placed. Push the threaded needle from the front of the garment (right side) to the back of the garment (wrong side) at this spot. **A**

**3.** Push the needle back through to the right side of the garment, spacing the stitch about as wide as the holes on the button. **B**

**4.** Put the needle through the underside of the button. **C**

**5.** Put the needle back through the button, this time on the top (right side), in the other hole. Put the needle through the top of the fabric just a few threads away from the first stitch you made. Pull the needle through to the wrong side, but don't tighten the thread so much that there is no wiggle room for the placket overlay. **D**

**6.** Repeat Steps 3–5 with 2–4 stitches for each set of holes or shank until the button is secure (this will depend on the weight of the fabric and button). Don't sew the button on too tightly. There needs to be enough room for the placket to sit comfortably below it. **E & F**

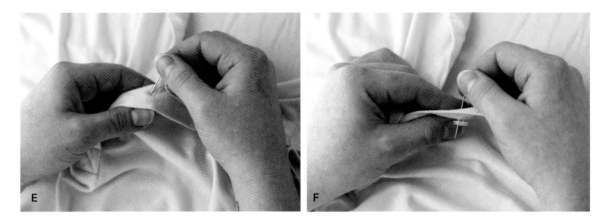

**7.** On the last stitch, don't pull the thread all the way through the button. Stop in the zone between the garment and the button, and tie a knot discreetly between the button and the placket. **G-J**

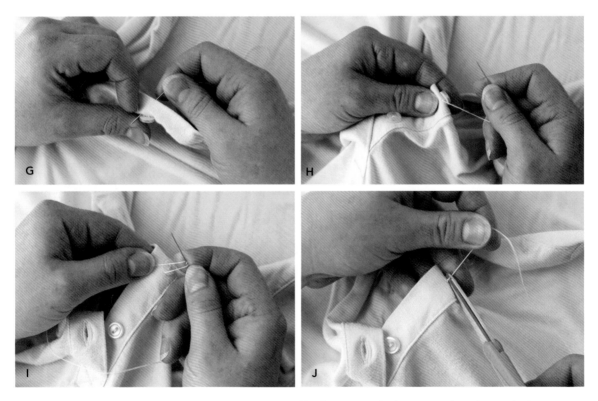

Now you should be able to button the garment smoothly, lining up the button with its buttonhole.

# Removing Stitches

Knowing how to take apart a garment's original seam (or undo your own sewing when you make a mistake) without damaging the fabric is an essential part of mastering wardrobe DIYs. Here are three ways of using a seam ripper to remove stitching:

## METHOD 1: BREAK EVERY FEW STITCHES ON ONE SIDE OF THE SEAM

Put the pointed end of the seam ripper under a stitch on the underside of the seam. Slide it through the stitch until the sharp blade in the trough of the hook cuts the thread. Cut through every third or fourth stitch of the bottom thread of the seam, and then turn the seam over and slowly pull off the upper thread. **A-E**

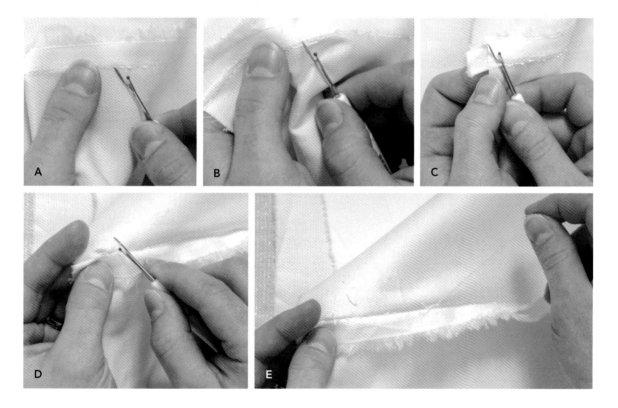

## METHOD 2: START WITH THE SEAM RIPPER, AND THEN GATHER WITH THE LONG THREAD

This method works best for longer stitches, light- or medium-weight fabric, and seams sewn with moderate or looser tension. In these situations, you can start by breaking some stitches on the underside for a few inches, as directed in Method 1. **A**

Then, grasping the long thread, pull slowly while holding the still-sewn fabric with your opposite hand, creating gathers in the fabric. Gather as much as you can until you feel the thread about to break; then use the seam ripper to cut the tight thread at the opposite end of the gathering. **B & C**

The entire thread will pull out, and you will have a long thread on the other side. **D**

On a long seam, you can try to take out the remaining stitches using a second long thread to repeat this process on the reverse side, but it may not work if the seam is too tight. In that case, pick out another few inches (several centimeters) on the wrong side and repeat the process until the seam is completely removed.

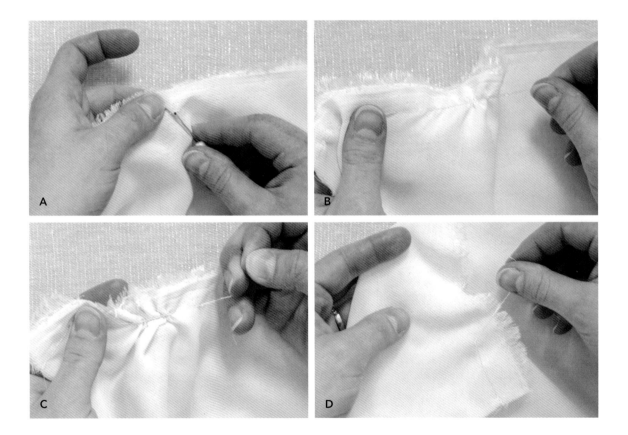

## METHOD 3: RIP THE THREADS DOWN THE CHANNEL BETWEEN SEAMS (A RISKY WAY TO USE A SEAM RIPPER)

The first two methods are examples of the right way to use a seam ripper. This third method is not ideal, but sometimes, with very thick thread and fabric, you have no choice but to rip some or all of a seam by slipping the long end of the seam ripper between the two fabric sides, wedging it under a stitch, and pushing until the stitch breaks, much like opening a letter with a letter opener. **A-C**

Once you're done, you'll have lots of tiny thread pieces to brush off. Use a lint roller if necessary. **D**

The reason this method is risky is that you can easily cut the sides of the fabric with the seam ripper, which is often irreparable. But if you plan to take in a seam considerably after unpicking it, you may choose to use this risky method to undo the seam more quickly.

You've been warned—try it at your own risk!

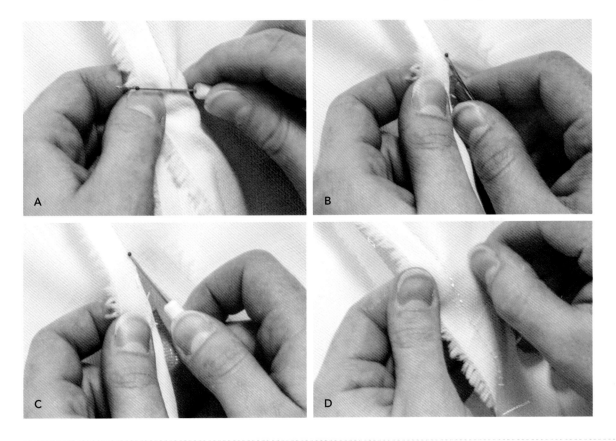

Regardless of the method, it's always a good idea to press the fabric again after you've removed the seam to remove the creases caused by previously stitching and pressing it.

# Hemming

One of the most important skills in mending and customizing clothing is taking out and putting in a new hem. There are many, many ways to put in a professional hem, including using the blind hem stitch (page 28). Three basic machine methods follow.

## METHOD 1: DOUBLE TURN-UNDER, TOPSTITCH

This produces the basic, common hem you see on most jeans, khakis, and button-up shirts, among other garments.

**1.** Fold up and press in place the raw edge of the fabric approximately ½″ (13mm) all the way around the bottom edge.

**2.** Fold and press up again with a deeper fold, concealing the raw edge. On pants, this should be 1″–1½″ (2.5–3.8cm). On a skirt or dress, it may be closer to 2″ (5cm). On lightweight garments or jeans, it may be just over ½″ (13mm).

**3.** Hold the folded hem in place with pins placed perpendicular to the hem edge.

**4.** From the wrong side, sew a straight stitch through all 3 layers (the first fold and the main fabric).

## METHOD 2: FINISHED EDGE, SINGLE TURN-UNDER, TOPSTITCH

Some fabrics are too thick or unruly to press under twice. This method produces a fast and easy hem that you can use in these situations.

**1.** Finish the raw edge of the fabric with a zigzag stitch (or a serger if you have one).

**2.** Fold up the fabric approximately 1″–1½″ (2.5–3.8cm). Press and pin in place.

**3.** Sew with a straight stitch.

This kind of hem works in a pinch and I sometimes use it for just the lining of a skirt, using Method 1 (at left) on the outer skirt.

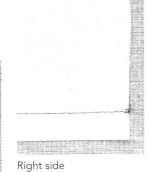

Right side                    Wrong side

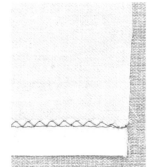

Right side                    Wrong side

# METHOD 3: SINGLE TURN-UNDER, TWIN-NEEDLE TOPSTITCH

This hem is the home sewist's version of a coverstitch hem, which is the hem you see on most store-bought T-shirts. Take a look at a commercial tee and you'll see two rows of straight stitches on the right side. Flip it over and on the underside you will see what looks like a braid of zigzags going between the rows. A special machine is used in the industry to quickly finish the raw edge and do the hemming all in one pass.

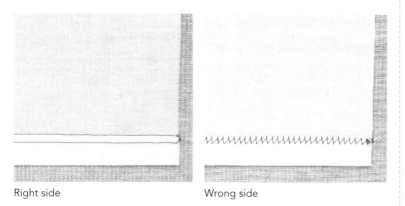

Right side                    Wrong side

We can use a standard sewing machine to get a similar result by utilizing a twin needle. With a "faux coverstitch," the zigzag stitch look comes from the bobbin thread traveling back and forth between two rows of straight stitching. The faux coverstitch hem is normally used for knits or other fabrics that don't ravel. This technique is used in Boxy Tee Makeover (page 150).

**1.** Follow your machine's instructions to insert a twin needle, and thread it using two spools of thread.

**2.** Fold and press up the raw edge 1″ (2.5cm), or as deep as you want the hem. Pin carefully.

**3.** With the garment's right side facing up, align the hem so that the raw edge of the hem allowance is directly under the twin needle and the stitches cover the raw (or serged) edge.

In Shorten a Pencil Skirt (page 62), you'll learn the blind hem, a more complicated technique. You may want to use that one again in Flared Pants to Skinny Pants (page 119) or any time you're rehemming tailored or dressier clothes. If you don't have a sewing machine, instead of a blind hem stitch you can hand sew an old-fashioned hem stitch, a type of whipstitch with a very short stitch on the front and a much longer stitch on the underside.

# Note

There are two ways to control the length of a garment you're hemming. If you want to make a garment shorter, remember that you'll have to keep enough length for whichever hemming method you use. So choose the method appropriate for your garment and fabric and add the extra 1″–2½″ (2.5cm–6.3cm) to the length you want before you cut off the excess fabric.

# Pressing

I talk a lot about pressing a seam allowance to one side, or pressing the fabric or garment flat before sewing the next seam. There is a difference between pressing and ironing.

Ironing is using an iron to remove wrinkles from a garment, using a sliding motion, and it's usually done to items after washing or unpacking them. Pressing is what we do while sewing, using an iron with an up-and-down motion and often working on only a small section at a time.

The way I see it, only about half of sewing is actually making seams. The rest is cutting out the pieces and pressing the seams you've just made. There is a clear difference between professionally made clothing and amateur attempts, not only in the seams but also in the way the garments lie. You can make your projects turn out twice as good just by taking the time to press each seam before moving on to the next one.

Throughout the book, I'll tell you when to press a seam or area before or after you sew. After you sew a seam (usually right sides together), you'll press the seam allowance open or to one side. Sometimes it makes a difference if you press the seam allowance to the left or right, or up or down, and the instructions will indicate the direction in those cases.

When you need to press a seam allowance *open*, the easiest way to get the fabric to cooperate is to press the seam allowance flat to one side first, and then use the point of the iron to spread apart the seam allowance and press the seam allowance open and flat. Pressing seam allowances open produces a flatter seam, although in some cases the thread may not be strong enough for seams that bear a lot of strain, such as the side seams on tight pants. In those cases, we press the seam allowance to one side, and sometimes even topstitch the seam allowance for extra strength and cooperation.

# Getting Out Wrinkles 101

- **Steaming and spraying:** For set-in wrinkles and for pressing sturdier fabrics, use the steam setting on your iron or a spray bottle filled with water to dampen the fabric before pressing.

- **Pressing cloth:** A pressing cloth is a napkin, handkerchief, or scrap of thin cotton or linen fabric that is used as a protective buffer between the iron and the garment when the garment is of a delicate fabric. It needs to be able to take high temperatures, so 100% cotton or linen is best. If any of the clothes you are reworking are made of wool, silk, or a textured fabric of any fiber (such as cotton corduroy or thick knit) be sure to use a pressing cloth to keep from making the fabric shiny and matted from the hot iron's pressure. You may also want to use a pressing cloth with a glossy, furry, or heat-sensitive fabric to protect the iron from any bits that might melt.

- **Iron temperature:** Refer to the temperature dial on your iron for specific settings, but remember the basics and trust your instincts since irons vary.

  Use low heat on polyester, acrylic, and other synthetic materials; these fabrics will melt when the heat is set too high.

  Use medium heat on wool and silk; these fabrics are delicate and can change in texture or color with too much heat or water.

  Use high heat on cotton and linen; these fabrics can take very high heat and more spraying. They also hold more wrinkles, so they may require extra pressing.

# How to Measure Yourself

Unless you're a pro at online shopping or sewing clothes for yourself, you may not know how to find key measurements on your body that you'll need to get a custom fit. For this book, the main measurement you'll need is your waist circumference, but it's good to know how to take all your basic measurements—they'll help you in your future DIY fashion endeavors!

You need a flexible measuring tape (page 21). Write down the measurements.

 **Tip** I recommend keeping your measurements in your phone or an online note-keeping tool so you always have them handy when you're in a store or cutting out a pattern.

**Bust** // Wrap the measuring tape around the widest part of your bust, keeping it parallel to the floor so it's not dipping lower in the back. Don't pull it extremely tight; take a breath while you hold it around yourself and make sure you can inhale with a little extra room.

**Waist** // Your waist is not the part of your torso where your pants waistband sits. It's actually the smallest part of your body between your bust and hips. Wrap the measuring tape around this point and pull it snug; this is your waist measurement.

**Hips** // Your hips are the largest part of your body below your shoulders, generally about 7″ (18cm) below your waist. You also need a little bit of room to move around with this measurement, since when you walk and sit your shape changes, so measure this circumference a little loosely (but not so loosely that the tape droops).

**Inseam** // This measurement is tricky to take by yourself, but you can do it if you work carefully. Starting at the crotch of your pants, measure down the inside of your leg to the point where you want the hem to fall. For cropped pants, this is generally right above the ankle bone; for flared pants, it may be near the top of the foot. I measure my own inseam by positioning the end of the tape measure on the inside of one leg at the crotch seam of my pants and holding it there with one hand, while I smooth the tape measure down my leg with the other.

**Skirt lengths** // When you make your own clothes, you get to pick the length and style, so you can make a mini, midi, maxi, or any length in between. Skirt length measurements are also a little hard to take by yourself, but use the same two-handed method to keep the measuring tape in place as you extend it down to the desired hem length. To measure your skirt length, I recommend measuring down the center of one thigh—as you bend down to reach the bottom of the hem point, walk your hands down from the top of the measuring tape so it doesn't move or shorten with you. You might want to have a friend help you with this. For some skirt styles, you may want your skirt length slightly longer in the back than in the front, so make a note of the lengths in both front and back if that's the case.

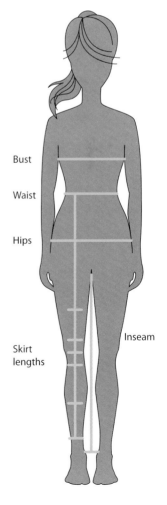

Bust

Waist

Hips

Skirt lengths

Inseam

# Sewing Commandments

I've come up with a few sewing do's and don'ts over the years that may help you as you begin your own wardrobe alterations and refashioning projects.

When in doubt, use a long stitch and check your work. If your seam is straight and the fabric pieces are lined up, just stitch over it with a regular-length stitch. But long stitches are easier to remove if you need to pull out the stitches and try again.

Clip threads near your backstitching after every seam (except when gathering). This will keep them from getting in your way as you make the next seams.

Don't sew over pins—certainly not over those pinned in line with the seam, but ideally not those perpendicular to the seam, either.

Channel your inner yogi while sewing and "find your center." In this case, it means the centers of your garment sections. Fold garments or pieces in half and snip a little triangle off at the top of the fold, which will leave a triangular notch marking the center front, center back, or middle of the side. These marks will enable you to line up waistbands, appliqué, or other parts of the garment when pinning and sewing. Finding the centers is especially important when gathering or working with very fitted clothing, since any asymmetry will be obvious. (See more about Centers, page 24.)

# Alteration Technique Tutorials

The techniques explained in this chapter are each simple projects. They're not dramatic design changes on their own, but these essential DIY techniques will enable you to alter clothing for fit and give you a strong foundation for doing more creative and complicated projects, such as those in the next chapter. You will learn to Take It In, Let It Out, Take It Up, and Let It Down.

# Take In a Sweater or Knit Top

This simple alteration project shows one of the most basic, but essential techniques I use. I often find sweaters are too boxy or shapeless, or that the waist is too high for my body. Adjust the side seams of these baggy sweaters with a few quick steps that make a huge difference. I've used this technique many times on cardigans, heavier-weight tees, and pullover sweaters to improve their fit.

## You Will Need:

- Loose or shapeless tee or sweater

- Standard sewing supplies

- Fabric pen or chalk *(optional)*

# Get It Done

**1.** Turn the sweater inside out and try it on. Pinch it in as desired at both side seams, approximately the same amount on each side. On one side, place several pins to mark where the narrowest point should be and where it should taper back to the original seam.

**2.** Press the sweater flat with an iron where you need to take in the seam. Move the pins if necessary to ensure that you capture an equal amount of fabric from the front and back sides and that the original seam is aligned along the side. Create a smooth line with the pins from the original side seam near the armpit to the narrowest point of the new waist, and down to the hip. Use a fabric pen if desired to connect the line between the pins.

**3.** Stitch along the pinned or marked line from the bottom edge of the sweater toward the armhole. Make sure to backstitch when you start and end the seam. (Be careful not to sew over the pins or you will break the sewing machine needle!)

**4.** Press the other side seam flat. Fold the sweater in half so the modified side seam is on top and copy the pin placement of the first side (now the seam) onto the second side. To do this, first match up the 2 sweater halves by aligning the top, bottom, and side seam edges and anchoring them together with a few pins. Be careful that the narrowest part (the waist) lines up, and that any darts begin and end at the same place on both sides.

Poke a pin from the first side through to the other side along the line of pins you placed on the seamline. Place pins in the spots where you poke to transfer the seamline so that the right and left sides of the sweater will be symmetrical. You can use a fabric pen to mark the "poke points" if you like.

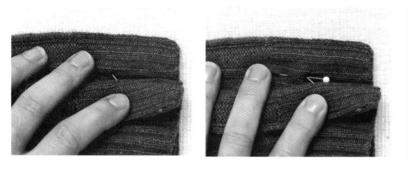

**5.** Press the new seam allowances toward the back of the sweater. They may be bulky, so press well on both the inside and the outside of the sweater. If you took in a large amount of fabric, you may want to trim the seam allowance, leaving about a ⅝″ (1.5cm) seam allowance. You can finish the raw edge with a zigzag stitch so that the seam allowance doesn't curl or unravel.

# Shorten Jeans

You can't always find a great pair of jeans with the perfect inseam—sometimes you're in between lengths, or there's no inseam choice. But if you've ever tried just cutting off the bottoms of your jeans and hemming them, you know that it never looks right. Jeans hemmed by the manufacturer have a worn-in look that is hard to replicate in a home sewing room. This clever technique creates a tuck just above the hem stitching line. The original hem is removed and the tuck is trimmed to less than $\frac{1}{2}''$, allowing it to be inserted into the hem allowance. When the hem is re-sewn, the tuck seems to disappear. You can keep the original hem and shorten the jeans to exactly the right length.

## You Will Need:

- Jeans that are too long

- Topstitch thread that matches the topstitching on the jeans

- Standard sewing supplies

# Get It Done

**1.** Try on the jeans. Mark with pins or a fabric pen where you want the hem to end.

**2.** Remove the jeans. With a seam ripper or pointy thread snips, take out the seam of the original hem on both legs. I recommend doing this by snipping every third stitch on the underside of the seam, and then pulling the top thread away in a single easy pull. (See Removing Stitches, Method 1, page 35.)

**3.** Press the bottoms of each leg flat. With a hem gauge or tape measure, measure and note the distance from the original bottom edge of the jeans to the mark or pins you added indicating where you want the new hemline to end. This is the length you'll want to remove. For example, this distance

will be 2″ (5cm) if the jeans are 2″ (5cm) too long. Remove the pins.

**4.** Fold up the bottom of the pants, right sides together. Locate the topstitching line of the original hem (on the right side of the jeans). Measure from the fold and adjust the folded amount until it is half the amount you want to shorten your jeans, plus about ⅛″ (3mm) extra room for the bulk of the hem. In this example, you'll measure 1″ (2.5cm) plus about ⅛″ (3mm) extra. . Pin evenly all around the leg opening.

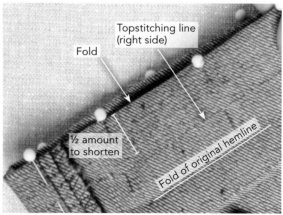

**5.** At the machine, stitch parallel to the original hem topstitching line, ⅛″ (3mm) away (on the inside of the folded tuck). If your actual tuck was more than ⅜″ (9mm) such as in this example, trim the tuck down to a ⅜″ (9mm) seam allowance so it can fit inside the original hem, presumably ½″ (13mm). Trim evenly around the fold line.

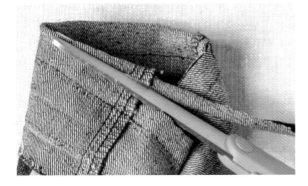

**6.** Turn the raw edge of the jeans back and press the new seam allowance down. It may be a little tricky to get the iron in there, but press well on the right and wrong sides of the fabric. You should still be able to see all 3 original creases / texture lines of the hem.

**7.** Fold the raw edge up along its original fold line, and then turn up again along the original hem fold. Make sure the trimmed tuck is concealed beneath the hem fold. Carefully pin through all layers all around the hem.

**8.** Stitch on the outside of the jeans leg so that you re-create the path of the original hem seam with your matching topstitch thread. Make sure to back-stitch when you start and end the seam, and use stitches similar in size to the rest of the topstitching on the jeans. You should be able to just barely see the seamline of the tuck ⅛″ (3mm) above the new hem seam. But it only shows up close!

# Let Out Pants Side Seams

Giving more room on tight seams is one of the simplest fixes you can make to improve fit on ready-made clothes. For some of us, jeans that fit in the hips and around the bottom are very tight in the thighs and calves. This trick, when done *correctly*, will produce a high-quality, comfortable result. Do this on pants or jeans that are a little too snug along the leg or even on the sleeves of a snug blouse or unlined jacket. It is a very simple way to get some necessary extra room!

## You Will Need:

- Jeans or pants that fit in the hips but are too snug in the legs

- Standard sewing supplies

# Get It Done

*Refer to Removing Stitches, Method 1 (page 39), for guidance.*

**1.** Turn the jeans inside out and use a seam ripper to pick out every second or third stitch of the outer seam. Leave alone the serger stitches that finish off the inside of the seam and keep the fabric from unraveling. (These stitches will hold the front and back pieces together before you sew a new seam.)

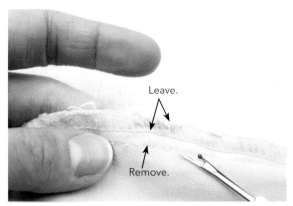

Leave.

Remove.

Pick out only the innermost straight line of stitches.

**2.** Stop ripping stitches a couple of inches (5cm) before you reach the hip at the top and the hem at the bottom. You will add a new stitching line that will taper to meet the old stitching in these areas.

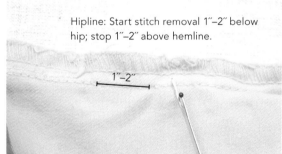

Hipline: Start stitch removal 1″–2″ below hip; stop 1″–2″ above hemline.

1″–2″

**3.** Carefully turn the pants right side out and try them on to make sure they aren't too loose with the extra space you just created. (Be gentle because the remaining serger seam is not reinforced and the serging isn't strong enough to stand up to much stress.)

**4.** Turn the pants wrong side out and pin the front and back together keeping them perfectly flat and paying special attention to the hip and hem areas so the original stitches don't come out. You will be sewing a seam inside the serger stitches along the leg where you needed more space, but merging into the original stitching at the hips and the hem. **A**

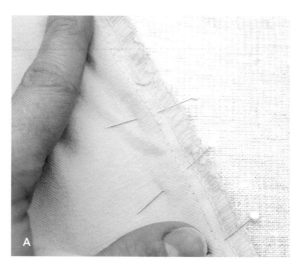

**5.** At the machine, stitch along the inner edge of the serged seam, effectively giving the pants a seam allowance the exact width of the serger stitching. This will reinforce the factory edge finishing and give you maximum room in the legs. (If the pants were a little too loose when you tried them on, you can sew somewhere in between the old seam and the edge of the serged seam.) **B**

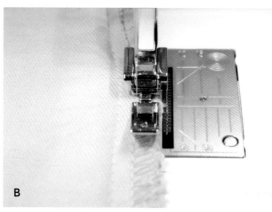

Sew just to left of serging for widest possible leg.

**6.** At the hip and hem of each side, merge the new seam with the original seam you left in. Create a smooth, straight line to prevent a bubble or pucker on the outside. **C**

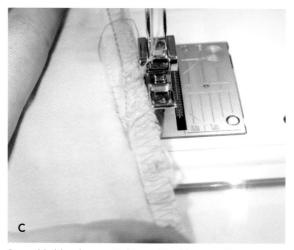

Smoothly blend new stitching with old seam allowance at hips and hem.

**7.** Once you've re-created the seams on both sides, turn the jeans right side out and spray with water. Press the seam on the highest setting available for the fabric content, being aware of the direction the seam allowance is facing (you may need to press it to the side with the jeans inside out first). Some jeans may show a line from the original seam, but this will become less noticeable with wear and washing, if pressing with water doesn't take it away completely.

# Take It Up

# Shorten a Curved-Hem Shirt

Many button-down woven shirts have curved hemlines and very shallow hems, so the basic methods for hemming (pages 39 and 40) are difficult to apply. But once you know the tricks for curved hemlines, you can alter these flattering tops with finesse! This one was almost tunic length on me and I wanted a more traditional length.

## You Will Need:

- Too-long button-down woven shirt

- Standard sewing supplies

## Note

Since the shirt hem is on a curve, a narrower hem will be easier to sew and will lie flat more easily. The shirt shown here is lightweight, so I used a very small (¼˝ (6mm)) hem. If your fabric is heavier, you may need to turn up the hem slightly more to accommodate the fabric's bulk. Try to re-create the depth of the original hem.

## Get It Done

*Refer to Removing Stitches (page 35) for guidance.*

**1.** Try on the shirt and mark the desired new length with pins, placing at least one pin at each side seam, center front, and center back. Take off the shirt, fold in half along the center front and center back, and pin together the left and right sides to keep them perfectly aligned.

**2.** Using a hem gauge and fabric pen, measure the length you plan to cut off along the entire bottom edge of half of the garment on the right side of the fabric. In the sample garment, that measurement is 3˝ (7.5cm). I also made ½˝ (13mm) marks below that, to accommodate a ¼˝ (6mm) hem.

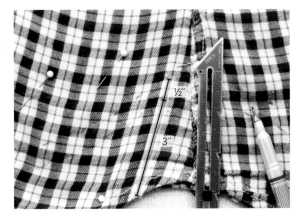

**3.** Cut along the bottom line you just drew, making sure both sides of the shirt stay in place.

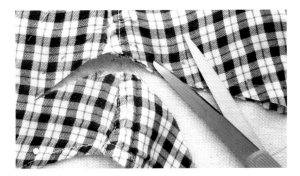

**4.** Fold up the raw edge ¼″ (6mm), press, and pin.

**5.** Sew in place using a long stitch. This stabilizing stitch won't show on the outside of the shirt when you're finished. Use pins and go slowly to keep the hem in line with the shirt.

Raw edge

**Tip** Normally with a basic machine hem you fold under twice and then sew, but in this case it is helpful to use a stabilizing stitch through the first fold because there is a curved edge. When fabric is cut on the bias or on a curve, the fibers stretch more than they do on the straight grain, and the hem can get distorted and stretched out as the feed dogs move it through the machine.. The stabilizing seam creates a nonstretchy, woven foundation for the curved hem.

**6.** Fold up the hem another ¼″ (6mm), press, and pin in place. The line you drew where you wanted the hem to finish should run along the bottom edge of the shirt now.

**7.** With a normal stitch length, sew through the pinned hem about ⅛″ (3 mm) from the bottom edge.

# Tighten a Loose Waistband

Gapping at the back waistband of a pair of jeans seems to be a very common problem. So often jeans don't follow our curves and the waistband is larger than we'd like, so there's extra room at the small of the back. Taking apart the waistband of jeans is not impossible (see Take In Jeans, page 70), but if you have less than 1″ (2.5cm) of extra room, all that work isn't necessary. Instead, this easier method snugs up the jeans in just a few steps. Your jeans waistband will hug more closely and match the great fit of the rest of the pants.

## You Will Need:

- Jeans that fit except for a gap at the waistband or center back

- 1" (2.5cm)-wide braided elastic (Length depends on the waist of the jeans and will be measured in Step 1.)

- Thread in a color that matches the jeans

- Standard sewing supplies

**Tip** Use *braided* elastic rather than *knitted* elastic because it's strong enough to pull together thick denim fabric.

# Get It Done

**1.** Cut a piece of elastic ¾ of the length of the back jeans waistband. For example, the jeans pictured measure 16" (40.5cm) across the back waistband, so I cut 12" (30.5cm) of elastic. Cutting a smaller ratio of elastic to make the jeans back waistband even tighter may result in awkward puckering above and below the elastic. **A**

**2.** Fold the elastic in half and mark the center point with a pin. Align that point with the center of the jeans back (at or between the center belt loop(s)). Hold the elastic in place with pins on either side of the center back on the inside of the waistband. Pin the ends of the elastic at, or near, the side belt loops, approximately centered on the height of the waistband (probably 1½"–2" high). **B**

**3.** Stretch the elastic out and add pins halfway between each side and the center back. This will ensure that the gathering power of the elastic is distributed evenly. **C**

**4.** At the machine with the right side of the jeans down and the elastic facing up inside the waistband, starting at either end of the pinned elastic, use a zigzag stitch to sew the top edge of the elastic in place. Stop sewing just before the center back belt loop when the needle is in a down position and backstitch. With the needle up and out of the fabric, raise the presser foot as you move the needle across the belt loop. Put the needle back down, backstitch, and resume sewing.

**5.** Sew another row of zigzag stitches on the bottom edge of the elastic, keeping the bottom edge parallel to the top edge of the elastic. Stitch this line of stitches just as you did the upper line in Step 4, skipping over the center belt loop and backstitching before and after the "jump." Snip the threads on either side of the center back belt loop on the right side and underside.

# Shorten a Pencil Skirt

Professional alterations may involve hemming techniques that are beyond the basics techniques used most often in this book. Tailors are extremely skilled with fine details and draping. But with a little patience and precision, we can replicate some of their techniques at home. This hemming project involves some basic tailoring, and it is very useful for those of us who need to hem dressier clothing for the office or an evening out. Just think of the money you'll save by mastering just a few skills!

## You Will Need:

- Too-long, unlined or partially lined skirt (or pants) in suit-weight wool or fine cotton (Use this technique for the outer skirt fabric and refer to Hemming, Method 1 (page 39) for guidance to hem the detached lining.)

- Fabric pen or chalk

- Standard sewing supplies

- Blind hem foot (recommended)

# Get It Done

*Refer to Removing Stitches, Method 1 (page 35) for guidance.*

**1.** Try on the skirt and place pins to mark the desired length.

**2.** Carefully pick out the original hem from the underside of the skirt using a seam ripper. Press open the old hem.

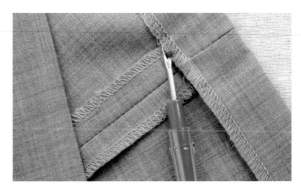

**3.** Add more pins in line with those you used to mark the hem and mark a straight line all the way around the skirt at the new bottom edge using a hem gauge to measure. You may also be able to use the fabric's grain as a guide to keep the pin line straight.

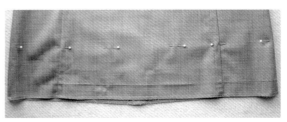

**4.** Mark 1½″ (3.8cm) below the pin line with a fabric marker or chalk. This will allow for a 1″ (2.5cm) finished hem (which is standard for tailored clothing) and a ½″ (13mm) turn-under.

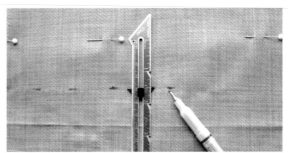

**5.** Cut along the drawn line.

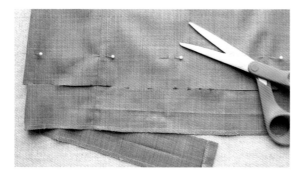

**6.** Fold the raw edge under ½″ (13mm) around the bottom edge and press.

**7.** Turn and fold under again 1″ (2.5cm); press and pin in place.

**8.** With the skirt still inside out, fold the hem allowance back toward the outside of the skirt and position on the sewing machine, exposing a small

⅛″ to ¼″ (3–6mm) folded top edge of the hem allowance. Using a blind hem foot if you have one, or a standard wide presser foot, use a blind hem stitch (page 28) to catch a few threads of the skirt (left) side every few stitches. Be careful to align the fabric evenly through the whole length of the hem, so the stitches on the outside are uniform. (If you prefer hand sewing, you can do a hem stitch by hand instead.)

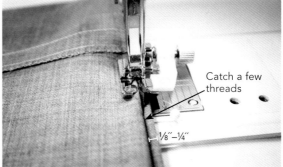

Catch a few threads

⅛″–¼″

# Lengthen a Skirt with a Hem Facing

Sometimes you need to make a skirt or pants just a little longer. If the garment has a deep hem (at least 1˝–2˝ [2.5–5cm]), you can do it. I made this miniskirt not so mini by opening up the hem and adding a hem facing on the inside so I could extend the skirt fabric to its fullest length. An inch or two may not sound like a lot, but sometimes it can make all the difference.

## You Will Need:

- Too-short skirt (or pants) with a deep hem

- ⅛ yard (12cm) coordinating prewashed fabric for inside facing

- Standard sewing supplies

# Get It Done

*Refer to Removing Stitches (page 35) for guidance.*

Like the facings used at armholes on sleeveless garments or along necklines when there is no collar, a hem facing finishes the edge of the skirt or pant leg with a seamline rather than a folded edge.

**1.** Using a seam ripper, carefully pick out the original hem from the inside of the skirt. Press open the old hem.

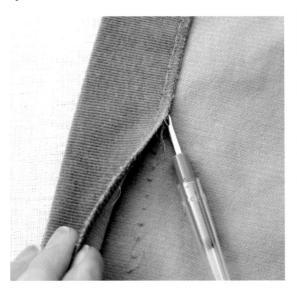

**2.** Place the skirt flat on top of 2 layers of the hem facing fabric. Cut out a hem facing, following the shape of the bottom of the skirt and allowing for a ½″ (13mm) seam allowance on the side seams. Mark the center front of the skirt and the hem facing.

Center front and back notches.

**3.** Use a hem gauge to mark the height of the hem facing along the entire piece. The height is equal to the height of the original hem plus 1″ (2.5cm) for seam and turn-under allowances. The original hem on the skirt pictured here was 1″ (2.5cm), so the height of my hem facing is 2″ (5cm) to allow for the ½″ (13mm) seam allowance and ½″ (13mm) turn-under. Cut along this line.

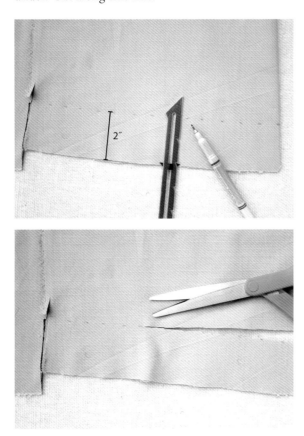

**4.** At the machine, stitch together the side seams with fabric right sides together using a ½″ (13mm) seam allowance. Press these seams open.

**5.** Along the top edge of the hem facing, fold under ½″ (13mm) and press.

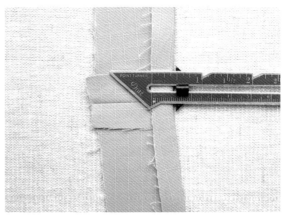

**6.** With right sides together, pin the hem facing to the outside of the skirt, matching the center back and center front notches. Stitch together using a ½″ (13mm) seam allowance.

**7.** On the inside of the skirt, press the seam allowance toward the hem facing. Flip to the right side of the skirt and press again.

**8.** Press back the hem facing toward the body of the skirt and pin in place. This hem should be the same depth as the original hem. For the skirt pictured, the hem was 1″ (2.5cm).

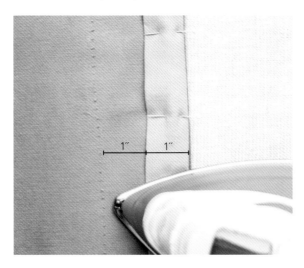

**9.** With the right side of the skirt facing up, top-stitch using a neat straight stitch, following the line of the original bottom edge of the skirt. This will disguise the fold line if you weren't able to press it completely out, and it will ensure that the hem is even all the way around.

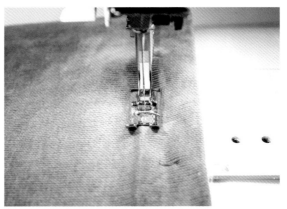

# Take It In:

# Take In Jeans

When a pair of jeans or pants is roomy beyond what a belt or a little elastic in the waistband can fix, you may have to do some denim surgery to make them fit the way you want. But it can be done! In this project you'll learn the steps to take apart structured pants or jeans and put them back together, good as new but an inch (2.5cm) or so tighter.

To change the size of the pants, you can take in the center back of the jeans, as is described here, or you can take in both side seams. I recommend you take in no more than 1″ (2.5cm) at any one place to avoid an odd bubble shape at the merged bottom of the seam.

This technique does involve a number of steps, but it's worth it to achieve a custom fit with a favorite pair of jeans or pants. For much-too-large pants you really want to salvage, try to take in the side seams; just make sure you take in the same measurement on both sides. (Taking in both side seams may be necessary if you need to take in more than an inch [2.5cm] or so, but it's twice the work of taking in only one place—the center back.) Taking the time to do every step correctly will make for a much more flattering pair of jeans!

## You Will Need:

- Too-big jeans or structured pants
- Topstitch thread in a color that matches the topstitching on the jeans
- Standard sewing supplies

For pants that are less than an inch (2.5cm) or so oversized in the back, refer to Tighten a Loose Waistband (page 59) for an easier fix.

# Get It Done

*Refer to Removing Stitches, Method 1 (page 35) for guidance.*

**1.** Use a seam ripper to unpick the stitches on the belt loop at the center back of the jeans. Make sure you grab the threads from the stitching without damaging the fabric of the jeans or belt loop.

**2.** Very carefully, pick out the topstitching on the back waistband of the jeans. Unpick the bottom and top edge stitches, about twice as far as you want to take in on either side. I wanted to take in 1″ (2.5cm) from the waist, so I unpicked about 2″ (5cm) of stitches on either side of the center back.

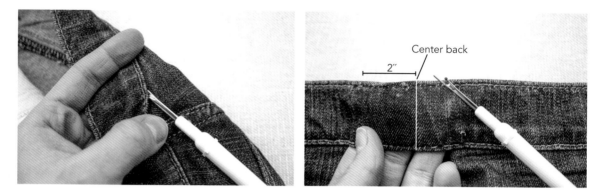

**3.** Remove the topstitching on the center back seam. Pick out several inches of the stitching, opening up the center back to the point where the jeans fit you. (In my case, this was the center of the seat; if you use this technique on side seams, you may have to remove the stitches all the way down to the thigh to make the jeans much smaller.)

**4.** Pin the center back seam back together—without moving the pieces to take it in—along the original seamline, aligning the original center seams. Be sure this alignment doesn't shift as you sew, or the new seam you put in may be off-center.

**5.** Using a long basting stitch, sew from the original jeans seam (the point to which you unpicked). Create the new center back seam, tapering out to the smallest point at the top of the waistband as you stitch. Create a smooth line or curve in the new seam as you take out the amount needed (no more than ½″ [13mm] if you want to take out the maximum of 1″ [2.5cm] I recommend for this seam). You may want to mark the point you're sewing to at the top edge. Try on the jeans after a first pass to see if you've taken out enough. Reshape the seam if necessary and deepen slightly if you need to take out more.

**7.** Press both sides of the seam allowance toward the narrow side. Press under the wide seam allowance ½″ (13mm) and pin it in place, folding over the smaller seam allowance.

**6.** If you made multiple seams while taking in the center back, pick out the unused stitches. Trim the excess fabric from the seam allowance, leaving a ½″ (13mm) seam allowance on one side and a 1″ (2.5cm) seam allowance on the other side, which you'll use to enclose the seam.

**8.** With matching denim thread in the bobbin, sew through all layers of the turned-under seam allowance from the inside.

**9.** On the outside of the jeans, with matching top-stitch thread as the top thread, sew the second row of topstitching on the center back seam, reinforcing the center back basting stitch and keeping the top-stitching parallel with the row you just made from the underside.

**10.** Next, take in the waistband. Cut down the center of the waistband in a straight cut. Turn these ends right sides together and pin.

**11.** Sew the waistband together. Some measuring may be required to make sure you take in the same amount from the waistband as you did from the center back. Cut off excess fabric if necessary, depending on how much you took in from the center back seam. Ideally, leave about a ½″ seam allowance.

**12.** Press this seam allowance open and press under on both edges to match the bottom edge of the waistband on the inside and outside.

**13.** With matching topstitch thread in the needle, topstitch along the top edge of the waistband, using pins if needed to keep the seam allowance pressed open.

**14.** Using pins inside and outside, pin the waistband to the pants and add topstitching to the bottom edge of the waistband, sandwiching the jeans between the top and bottom waistband pieces, fully aligned.

# Simple Fix for Mending Jeans

This tutorial is the most popular one on my blog, and I've used this essential technique many, many times on several pairs of jeans. Here's a summary of my Simple Fix for Mending Jeans, plus some tips on how to use it for particularly tricky holes.

We all have favorite jeans, the pair that is so perfectly worn in that you can't duplicate the softness and fit—but what happens when you wear a hole through them? It's time to do a little patchwork.

## You Will Need:

- Beloved jeans with a hole
- Thread to match the denim color
- Fusible interfacing—enough to cover holes
- Standard sewing supplies

# Get It Done

**1.** Gather your interfacing. I recommend the nicer polyester Pellon type. Scraps from larger projects work well for this.

**2.** Turn the jeans inside out and assess the damage. Cut a piece of interfacing large enough to generously cover the hole and place it on top.

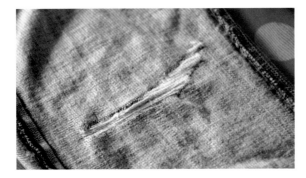

**3.** Set the iron for cotton and fuse the interfacing to the inside of the jeans. Make sure the entire hole is covered. If the jeans have spandex in them or are stretched out around the hole, you may want to pin them to the ironing board when you press the interfacing so you maintain the original shape of the jeans leg.

Stretch jeans pinned flat

**4.** Turn the jeans right side out and position them under the presser foot of your sewing machine. It can be pretty awkward to get the pants in the right position, depending on their size and the location of the hole. Using blue or white thread to match or blend with the jeans, sew forward, backward, forward, backward, aligned with the fabric grain over the hole. Repeat many times until the hole is patched and the interfacing is well attached.

# A Couple of Options for Tougher Holes...

- If the threads are missing and the hole is literally gaping, add a piece of lightweight cotton behind the interfacing to strengthen the fix.

- Because the interfacing may loosen after multiple washings, you can stitch an oval once around the edge of the patch to secure all four sides, but be aware that the stitches against the grain will be more noticeable.

- To mend jeans when the holes are in the knees, you'll have to slide the jeans leg onto the machine's arm and rotate the leg so it is parallel to the path of the needle. I like to cuff up the jean once or twice so it's flat and can fit under my presser foot when I lift it as high as it goes. Then hold the jeans in that parallel position while you sew back and forth as you would do on a hole in any location.

**I still get a lot of wear out of jeans I've mended this way!**

# DIY Style Projects

This chapter will show you how to use the techniques from the first parts of this book to take your DIY projects to the next level—remaking and redesigning your clothes. With the basics shown in Sewing Skills (page 30) and Alteration Technique Tutorials (page 45) plus a wider range of original garments and a little creativity, you can make all sorts of one-of-a-kind, upcycled DIY items that suit your personal style. This chapter presents many of my faves!

The projects generally fall into three categories: Refashion, in which a garment is made over into another type of garment, such as a shirt into a skirt; Remake, in which an item is made more interesting, personal, fashionable, or flattering; and Embellish, adding fun flair to a piece to decorate it in a stylish way.

# Infinity Scarf Makeover

This is one of my favorite sewing projects. It's perfect for both the beginning DIYer and the advanced sewist. While fringed scarves are a great basic by themselves, I am a fan of the more recent trend of infinity scarves that loop around without ends. This project turns an old, tired fringed scarf into a chic infinity scarf and teaches you how to make French seams, a classic sewing technique. French seams are beautiful, quality seams that hide raw edges without the need for a lining or edge stitch.

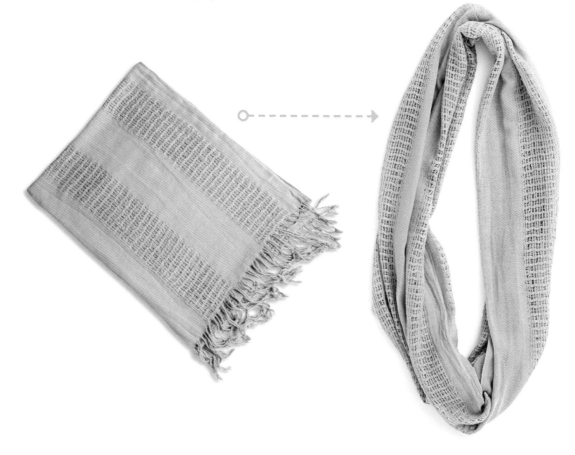

## You Will Need:

- Basic woven scarf

- Standard sewing supplies

# Get It Done

**1.** Fold the scarf in half crosswise, bringing together the fringed sections. If the scarf has a pattern or print that gives it a right and wrong side, make sure you fold together the *wrong* sides for this seam, which should face inside at this stage. Pin and sew a straight seam ¼″ (6mm) from the finished edge of the scarf (ignoring the fringe).

**2.** Trim off the fringe pieces, very close to the end of the scarf. This is important because any little bits of fringe you leave could poke through the next seam when you're done.

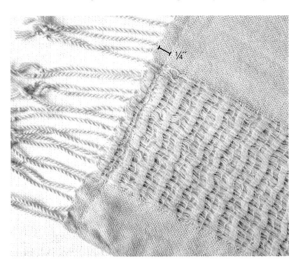

**3.** Open up the scarf and press the seam allowance to the side. Turn it over so the raw-edge side is facing down, and press again.

**4.** Fold the scarf in half again, placing the seam right at the edge of the fold. The scarf will now have its right sides together (if the fabric has right and wrong sides). With the seam centered along the new folded edge, press and pin through the seam allowance to keep it in place.

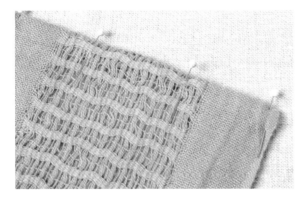

**5.** Sew the new fold closed using a ⅜″ (9mm) seam allowance. This will enclose all of the fringe trimmings.

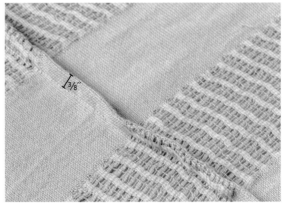

**6.** Press the new seam allowance to the side, and then flip it over and press from the outside.

# Colorblock Sweater Makeover

Put together two sweaters or tees to make the best of each of them. I used the sleeves from a sweater I was no longer crazy about, and the body of a sweater I liked but wished had full-length sleeves.

If you like this technique, make several and play around with where you place the colorblocks. How about contrast sweater cuffs, or a colorblock band under the bust, in the middle of the torso, or halfway down the sleeves? You could even experiment by combining three tees!

## You Will Need:

- Two sweaters, knit tops, or tees (both should be the same size, gauge, and weight)

- Standard sewing supplies

- Walking foot (recommended)

# Get It Done

**1.** Try on the main body sweater and mark with a pin the place on the sleeve where you want the colorblocking to begin. Place both sweaters flat on a surface. Align the sweaters at the neck edge and both shoulders. The arms, laid flat, should be the same width and size. Press them flat if necessary.

**2.** Place more pins on the sleeve, following the knit rows of the sweater to mark a straight line. Using a hem gauge as a guide, measure an additional ½″ (13mm) from the pinned line toward the cuff, and mark. Cut off the bottom of the sleeve.

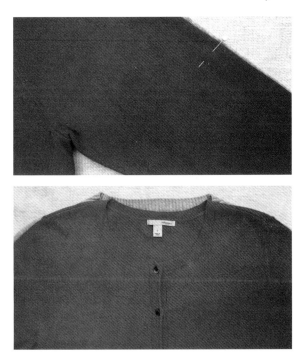

**3.** Move the pins to the sweater you are using for the new sleeves, and mark the new cut line. Measure 1″ (2.5cm) up from this line and cut off the sleeve.

**4.** On both sweaters, fold in half, and duplicate the straight lines you just cut on each sleeve onto the opposite sleeves.

**5.** Keeping the new sleeve right side out, turn the body sweater inside out and position the new sleeve inside it, right sides together, matching the long seams along the underside of the arm. Pin the sleeve in place.

**6.** At the machine, using a walking foot if possible to avoid stretching the knit, stitch together the sleeve sections, leaving a ½″ (13mm) seam allowance.

**7.** Press open the seam allowances.

**8.** Turn the sweater right side out. Using thread that matches the body sweater, topstitch the open seam allowance on the body side.

**9.** Using thread that matches the sleeve side, topstitch the open seam allowance on the sleeves.

# Contrast-Sleeve Tee

I like the trend of contrasting sleeves, but I'd much rather remake tees I already have than buy new ones. This project is an easy way to transform a basic, boring, short-sleeved crewneck tee into something way more fun. Try this with two loose tees, two lightweight tees, or two stretch tees for different looks and silhouettes. What a clever way to salvage a tee with a great texture or color when part of it gets stained or damaged!

## You Will Need:

- Two tees, same size and fit
- Standard sewing supplies
- Walking foot (recommended)

# Get It Done

**1.** On both tees, carefully cut away the sleeves, leaving the serged seam allowances on the body side of the tee.

**2.** Matching the shoulder seams and underside seams of the sleeve and armhole, pin together the right sides, turning the tee inside out and keeping the sleeve right side out.

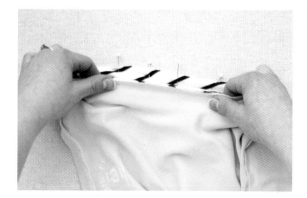

**3.** At the machine, use a walking foot to prevent excess stretching, and stitch just inside the original serged seam on the main tee. (This is probably between ¼″ [6mm] and ⅜″ [9mm]).

**4.** Press the seam allowances toward the sleeves.

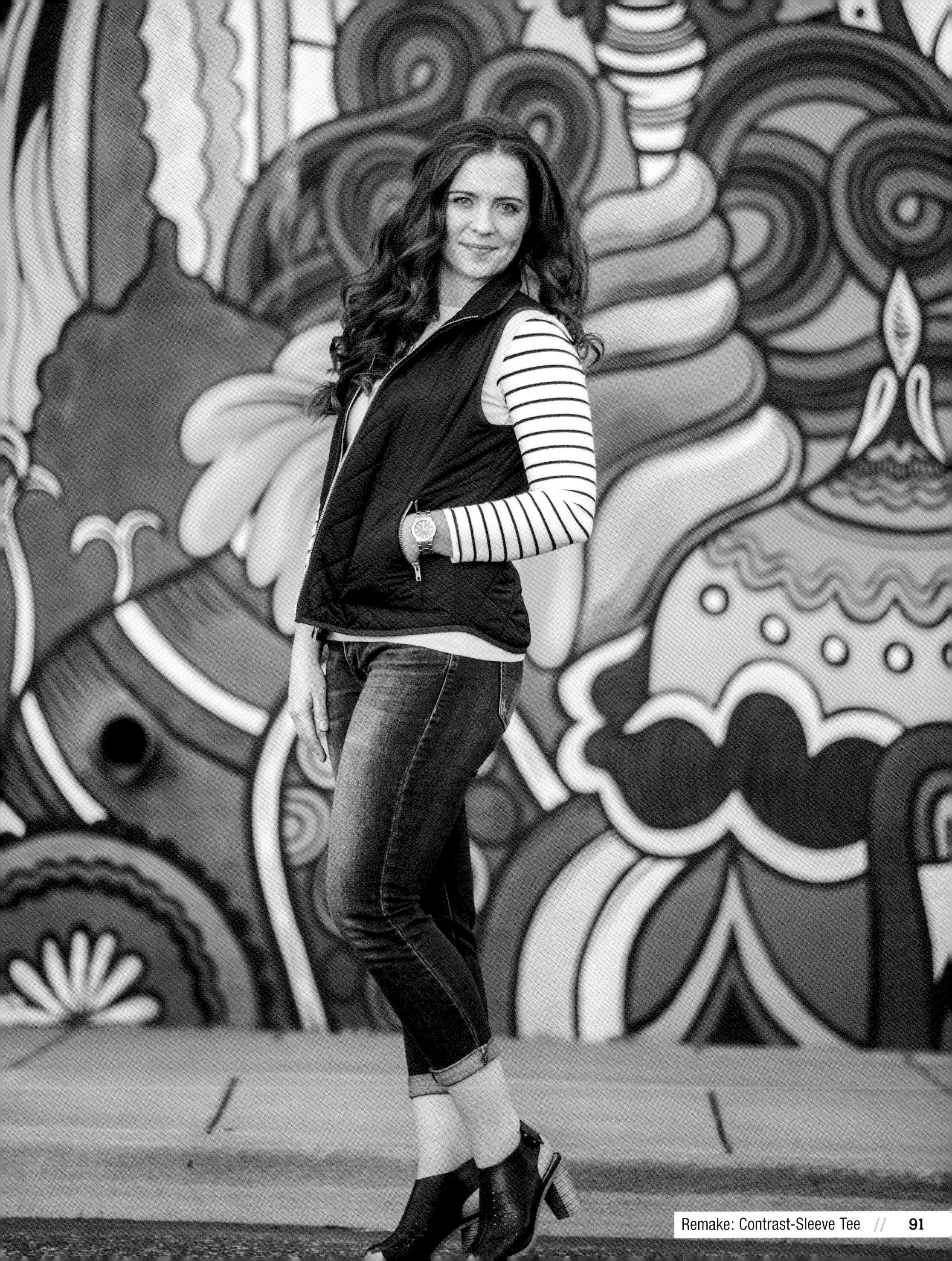

# Elbow Patch Sweater Makeover

I often find that the elbows of my fine-gauge sweaters get stretched out with wear, so sometimes I sew on a custom patch detail to prevent damage and add interest. You can do this with a lightweight leather patch on a heavier sweater, or use contrasting fabric. For a classic look, add patches to a jacket that's getting worn down in the elbows. And think beyond ovals—heart-shaped patches are cute and circles are fun. The one rule is that the patch fabric shouldn't be much heavier than the sweater fabric or it will pull on the sweater sleeve.

## You Will Need:

- Light- or medium-weight sweater, jacket, hoodie, or tee

- Coordinating fabric: about ⅛ yard (12cm) (prewashed)

- Heat*n*Bond Lite Iron-On Adhesive: about ⅛ yard (12cm)

- Standard sewing supplies

## Get It Done

**1.** Try on the sweater and place pins on either side of your elbow to mark where the patch will go. Lay the sweater flat and find the same points on the other arm. Press the sleeve flat.

**2.** Cut 2 rectangles of fabric the approximate length and width for the patch. Cut 2 pieces of a similar size out of the Heat*n*Bond.

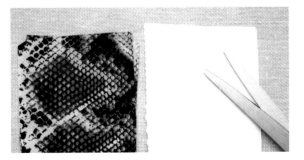

**3.** Iron the Heat*n*Bond rectangles to the fabric rectangles, following the manufacturer's instructions. Use a pressing cloth or Teflon pressing sheet to prevent a sticky mess on your iron or ironing surface.

**4.** Cut the patch into the desired shape. Position it on the sleeve and check for placement, size, and shape. Cut a second identical patch. Try on the sweater to confirm the placement before you iron it down.

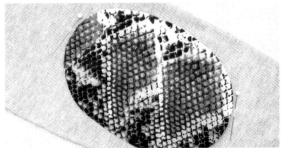

**5.** Peel the paper backing off the patch and iron it onto the sleeve.

**6.** At the machine, sew on the patch with a straight stitch or a short zigzag stitch that covers the patch edge. (Because my sleeves were a tight fit on the machine, I used a straight stitch. If I'd had more maneuvering room, I could have used a zigzag stitch with more precision to cover the raw edges of the patch.)

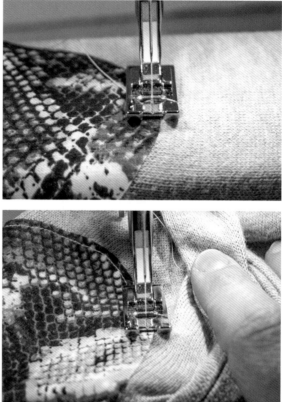

# Riding Pants Makeover

I have no need for functional equestrian riding pants, but I like their edgy knee-patch styling so I made my own from basic skinny pants. Give old pants a totally new look just by adding patches! Try fun colors and go completely cool and casual, or make the patch from leather for a chic, urban vibe.

**Tip** Maneuvering narrow pant legs on the free arm of a sewing machine can be a challenge, so you might want to first try the simpler Elbow Patch Sweater Makeover (page 92).

# You Will Need:

- Skinny pants
- Fabric: about ⅛ yard (12cm) (prewashed)
- Heat*n*Bond Lite Iron-On Adhesive: ⅛ yard (12cm)
- Standard sewing supplies

# Get It Done

**1.** Cut the approximate shape and size for the knee patches out of the fabric. Mark the patch placement on the knees and inner leg of the pants with fabric pen, chalk, or pins.

**2.** Cut 2 pieces of a similar size and shape as the fabric out of the Heat*n*Bond. Iron it to the fabric, following the manufacturer's instructions. Use a pressing cloth or Teflon pressing sheet to prevent a sticky mess on your iron or ironing surface.

**3.** Cut the patch and adhesive into the desired shapes. If the interfacing isn't completely secure, press it in place again.

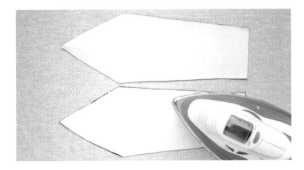

**4.** Peel off the backing and position the patch on the pants. Press in place, and repeat on the other leg.

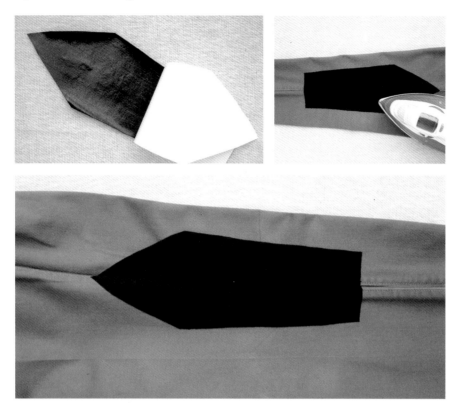

**5.** Using a short, wide zigzag stitch, finish the edges of the patches all around.

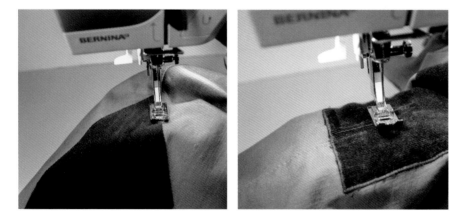

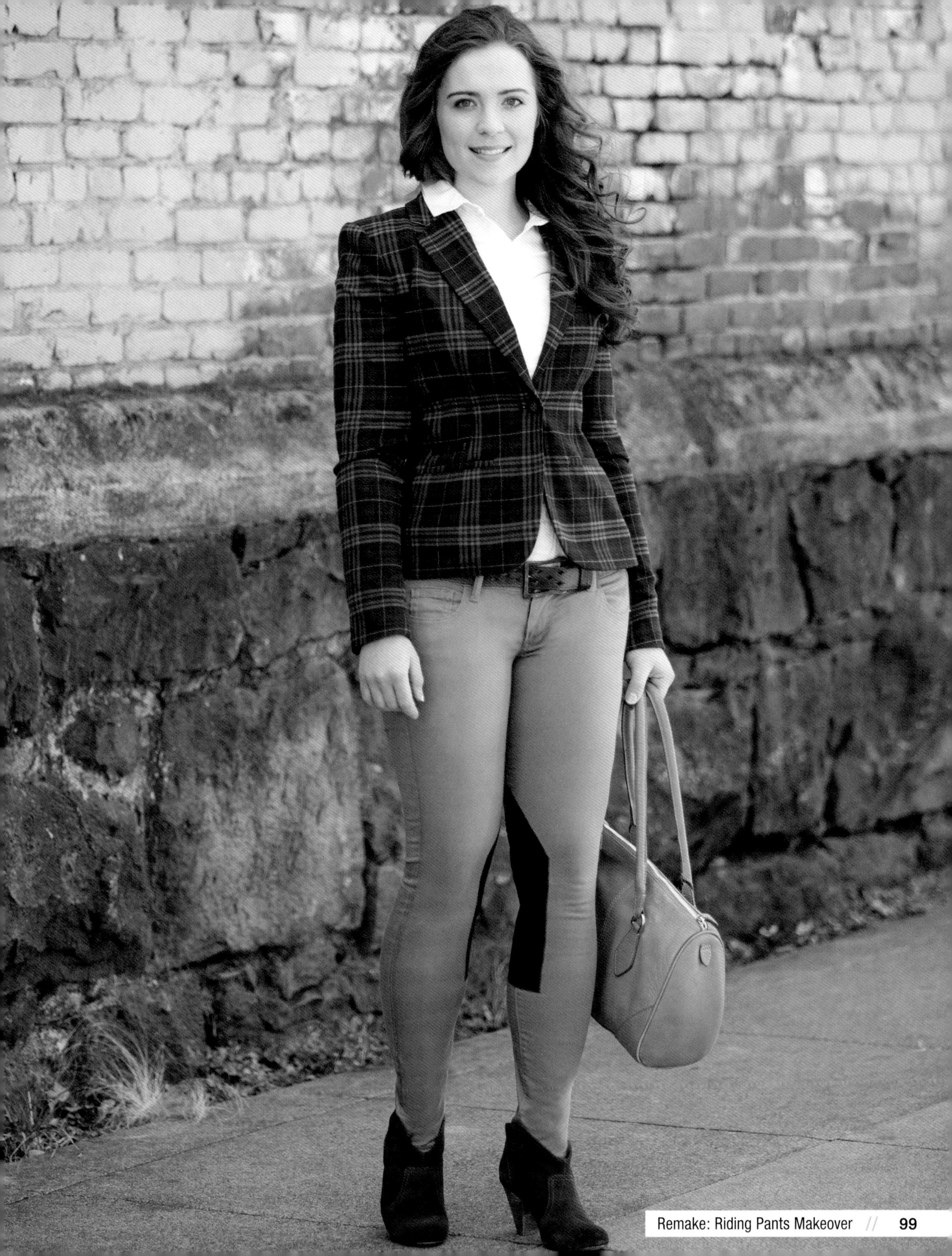

# Dress-into-Peplum-Top Makeover

Take a knit minidress that you never wear and transform it into a fitted peplum top. This project is a great way to salvage a dress that's a little too short, like the gray dress featured on the cover! This is a true refashion. You'll end up with a comfy peplum top or tee with custom waist and peplum lengths.

## You Will Need:

- Straight (no waist seam) dress or tunic (or tee and extra fabric)
- Lingerie elastic or other light-weight elastic
- Fabric pen or chalk
- Standard sewing supplies

# Get It Done

*Refer to Removing Stitches (page 35) for guidance.*

**1.** Try on the dress and find where it hits your natural waist (or wherever you want the peplum to begin). Place pins on either side to mark the desired position.

**2.** Make sure both sides match and mark the waistline of the new top, using a quilting ruler and fabric pen. Cut ½″ (13mm) below the marked line.

**3.** Try on the tunic bottom or dress skirt you just cut off. Hold it up around your waistline, and decide where you want the hemline to fall. Place a pin at this point on both sides. Lay the skirt flat, make sure both sides match, and cut ½" (13mm) above the desired waistline.

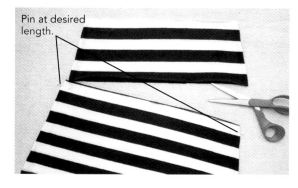

Pin at desired length.

**4.** Measure and cut a piece of elastic approximately 90% the circumference of the dress at the waistline. In my case, the width of the dress (flat) was 14" (35.5cm), so I doubled that to get the total waist circumference, 28" (71cm). I cut a piece of elastic 25" (63.5cm) long.

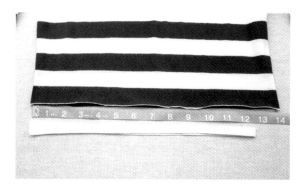

**5.** At the machine, sew together the elastic, forming a smooth loop and overlapping the 2 ends by about 1" (2.5cm). I do this by sewing a rectangle along a side of the elastic; make sure you sew against and along the grain of the elastic to secure it from pulling out later.

**6.** Fold both the bodice and skirt pieces in half lengthwise and cut notches to mark the center front and center back on both pieces. Using a very long stitch and tight tension, sew a gathering stitch (page 28) all the way around the skirt piece of the dress with about a ⅜" seam allowance.. Do not backstitch, and leave the ends of the threads long. Pull gently on both ends of the top thread to create gathering.

# Bonus: Peplum Variations

There are lots of silhouettes and styles you can play with when making your peplum top. Depending on the weight and pattern of the dress, you might find that a shorter, more ruffled peplum looks better, or that something a little more structured is more wearable. There are several simple ways you can modify this project to suit the dress you have and style you're aiming for. Here are my faves:

- Skip the elastic step and just press (or zigzag topstitch) the seam allowance and gathers toward the bodice for a looser look.

- Rather than cutting off the dress just below your natural waist, try a dropped waist look and cut it off a few inches below (try it on first to find the right placement). You can take in the side seams from the waist down if you have some extra room so that the top fits straight to the peplum seam. (I used these first two variations on the top on the cover of this book!)

- Create an empire waisted top (perfect for maternity or hot summer days) by attaching the skirt just below the bust and leaving a much longer skirt.

- Instead of gathering the bottom portion of the skirt, create pleats (matching on both sides) and pin or baste in place before attaching to the bodice.

- For a fuller peplum, use a contrasting fabric and create the skirt in any size and length you want (use one of the hemming techniques, page 39). I recommend a similar weight fabric to the dress you use, so the peplum lays nicely and doesn't tug at the bodice too much.

**7.** With right sides together, match the center front, sides, and center back of the gathered skirt and main dress body and sew, arranging the gathers evenly. Use a ½" (13mm) seam allowance.

**8.** Press the seam allowance toward the main dress body.

**9.** Aligning the center front, sides, and center back of the elastic and dress, pin, and sew the elastic through the seam allowance and main dress body using a wide zigzag stitch.

# Contrast-Trim Blazer

The contrast edge-trimmed blazer look is preppy and fun, and you can do it yourself using any color of double-fold bias tape as the trim and any blazer or jacket you have. You can add this kind of trim to anything, really—imagine it on a lightweight trench coat, a miniskirt, or the legs of shorts. Bias tape comes in many, many colors, so you have lots of possibilities.

# You Will Need:

- Blazer, jacket, or other structured garment

- ½″ (13mm) double-fold bias tape in a contrasting color

- Standard sewing supplies (sewing machine recommended, or you could hand sew using a small, neat whipstitch to attach the binding on the outside and the underside)

# Get It Done

*Refer to Stitch in-the-Ditch (page 28) for more information.*

**1.** Open up the bias tape and find the slightly narrower half. We'll call this the "right" side. Pin the right side of the bias tape to the right side of the blazer, beginning at the center back pleat opening and leaving 1″ (2.5cm) of bias overhanging the leading edge. Pin very carefully at the curves.

**2.** Sew the tape to the jacket, stitching through the fold in the tape. Stitch all the way around to the point in the front where the lapel turns back (near the highest button). Cut the bias tape at this point. Do this on both the right and left sides.

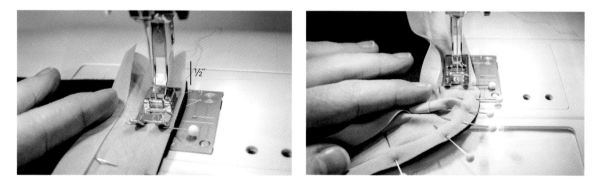

**3.** Press back the seam allowance and the wrong side of the tape into their folded position over the edge of the garment, and pin. At the bottom of the center back pleat opening, fold the open tape back on itself before you fold the "inner" side of the tape down.

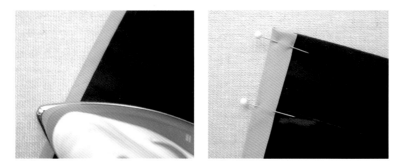

**4.** From the outside, stitch in-the-ditch between the bias tape and the lapel with thread that matches the blazer, catching the wider side of the double-fold bias tape on the back. Stitch slowly and carefully at the curves. You may have to pin in tiny pleats as you go.

**5.** At the points where the lapels fold backward (at the bottom pin), pin the bias tape with the narrower "right" side to the right side of the lapel. Note that this had been the wrong side for the first application of the bias trim. Fold over about ⅜" (9mm) of the short end of the bias to conceal the raw edge, and overlap the raw edge of the existing trim.

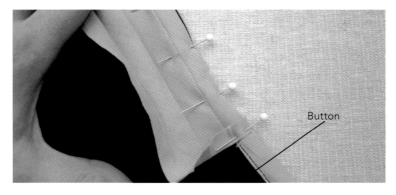

Button

**6.** As you did before the lapel-turning point, sew through the fold of the bias tape. At the corner of the carefully pinned lapel, stop sewing straight in from the point. Backstitch. Remove the needle from the work. Move the bias tape behind the needle, return the needle to the corner point, pivot at the corner, backstitch, and resume sewing.

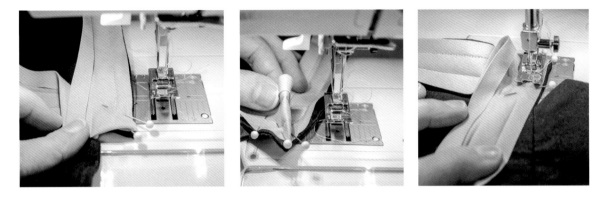

**7.** At the inside corners of the lapels, stop sewing and cut off the bias tape, leaving about ⅜″ (9mm) to turn back. Sew it down through the fold of the bias tape. **A**

**8.** Keep sewing, aligning the bias tape with the edges of the lapel as you go. (Start with an extra ⅜″ (9mm) folded under—the reverse of the edge treatment you just did.) Sew all the way around the collar to meet the other side's lapel turning point. Repeat Steps 3 and 4. At the corner points, keep the bias tape open until you sew to the inside corner; then flip under the wider side of the bias tape, pin, and resume sewing (this creates a mitered corner). **B**

**9.** At the inner corners, lift the presser foot, move to the next lapel, and resume stitching in-the-ditch. When you're finished, snip the threads between the stitch in-the-ditch seams. **C**

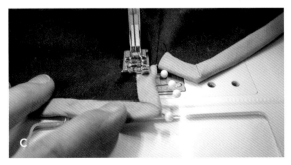

# Flared Pants to Skinny Pants

For years I have been transforming bootcut or flared dress pants into matchstick-straight pants. I found I could give old wardrobe staples a second life as flattering and fitted pants that are great for the office or more formal looks. This transformation will make the most out of shopping your closet for brand new pants.

Most trousers are easy to work with since their side seams don't have topstitching to pick out. If you want to do this project with jeans, see Variation for Jeans (page 116).

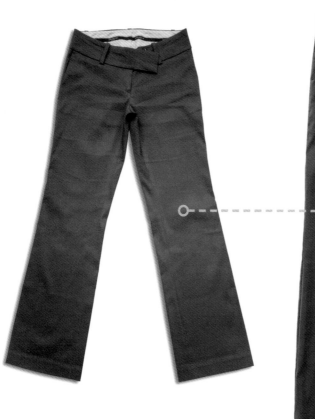

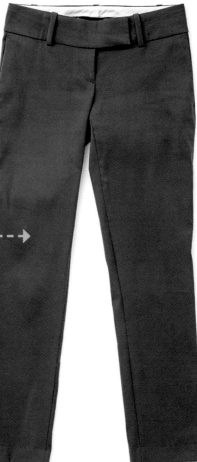

## You Will Need:

- Bootcut, wide-leg, or flared pants (or jeans)
- Standard sewing supplies
- Pinking shears (recommended)
- Fabric pen or chalk *(optional)*

# Get It Done

*Refer to Removing Stitches (page 35) for guidance.*

**1.** Turn the pants inside out and put them on. Place pins along the side seams to mark how fitted you want the legs to be. (Ask a friend to help pin if necessary.) Take equally from the front and back, keeping the old seam allowances centered and folded smoothly together.

Keep the centerline of the pant legs straight while you pin, even if it means taking in more from a single seam than the other on each leg. Pin all the way up to the point on the knee or thigh where the pants fit correctly, tapering the pins in a smooth line from the tightest point to the original seam. At the bottom, mark where you want the pants to end—flared pants are often longer than straight ones, which may end just at the ankle bone.

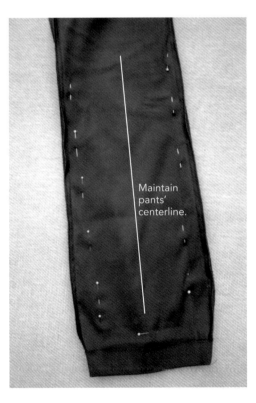

Maintain pants' centerline.

**2.** Make sure the pin placement is even. Use a fabric pen if desired to connect the line between the pins from the original seam to the hem. Pick out the hems of both legs with a seam ripper.

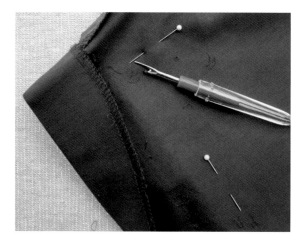

**3.** Sew along the lines of your pins, tapering from the original seam to the point on the knee or thigh where the pants fit correctly. Remove the pins as you work, being careful not to sew over them. Repeat on the other side of the same leg.

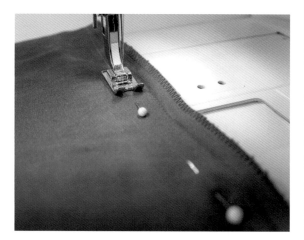

**4.** Trim off the excess fabric, leaving about a ½" (13mm) seam allowance on both sides. Try on the pants and make sure you like the fit of the first leg. If it's still loose, taper slightly more on the loosest side, and then try them on again.

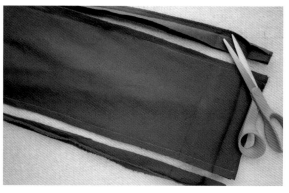

**5.** Once you know you like the fit, use the first leg as a pattern for the second by folding the pants in half and aligning both legs, matching up the grain and seam allowances at the thigh where you began tapering the seams. Pin together.

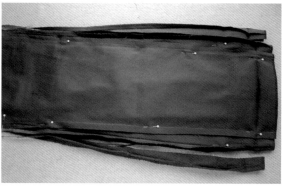

**6.** Cut off the same amount of fabric from the second leg as you did from the first, pinning right sides together to form the new seam allowance as you go, keeping the front and back perfectly lined up.

**7.** Sew the second leg seams with a matching ½″ (13mm) seam allowance.

**8.** Starting at the bottom of the pant legs, trim the raw edges of both seam allowances with pinking shears until you reach the original serged edges.

**9.** Pick out the original side seams with a seam ripper to the point where you began tapering.

**10.** Press open all side seams.

**11.** Try on the pants again and double-check the length. Determine where you want the hemline and place a pin or make a mark with a fabric pen.

Dressier pants like these typically have a blind hem. More casual cotton pants or jeans normally have a straight hem stitch. Re-create the hem stitch appropriate to your pants.

To re-create the depth of the original hem (usually about 1½″ [3.8cm]), measure 1½″ (3.8cm) down from the desired length you pinned. Cut off the excess on both pant legs.

If your pants originally had a turned-under hem, as some lightweight cotton pants do, re-create the original hem by adding a 1″ (2.5cm) turn-under and turn it under ½″ (13mm) twice (see Hemming, Method 1, page 39) rather than using the edge finishing stitch described in Step 11.

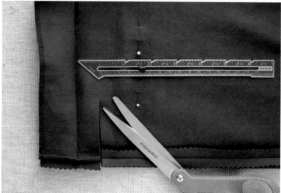

**12.** Finish and reinforce the cut edge of the bottom with an overlock stitch, which combines zigzag stitching with a straight stitch and functions like a serger finish.

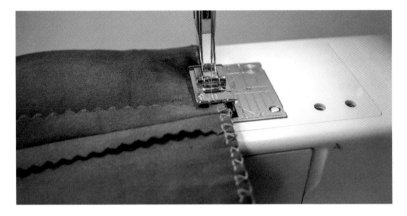

**13.** Press under 1½″ (3.8cm), using a hem gauge to measure, and pin.

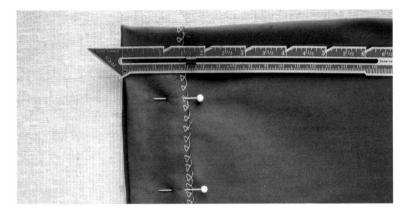

**14.** Hem the pants using a blind hem stitch (page 28).

**15.** Press flat.

# Bonus: Variation for Jeans

I first turned a pair of boot cut jeans into skinny ones in 2009, with great success. I realized what a valuable skill it was when I had a dresser full of flared jeans but wanted to try the skinny jean trend! Since then I've turned boot cut jeans into straight ones as well, and learned I can manipulate the legs to the shape I want by trying them on while sewing and tapering them gradually.

Jeans are constructed differently than khakis or dress pants, so taking them in requires some changes from the previous project. You may recognize these jeans from the cover of this book!

## Instructions

**1.** The biggest difference between jeans and tailored pants is that the inseam of jeans is usually top-stitched. You'll need to remove the top stitching to get the layers to lay flat, and you'll have to replace it to make the jeans look normal when you're done taking them in. Do this part first, removing the stitching from the top of the flared portion of the legs.

**2.** Now you can turn the pants inside out and try them on, marking the approximate locations of the seams and hem with pins—exactly as you did in the pants project.

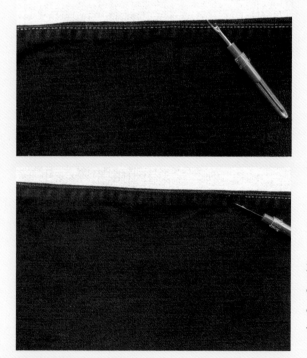

**3.** You'll probably have several inches (centimeters) of extra fabric at the bottom of the jeans, since boot cut or flared ones are often much longer than skinnies, which you probably want to end around the ankle bone. But just to be safe, cut off the original hem of the jeans leaving as much room as possible, cutting evenly and parallel to the original hem all the way around.

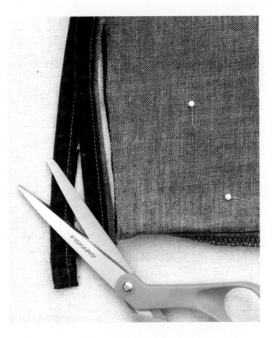

**4.** Once the top stitching and original hem are removed, the process for making jeans skinny is pretty similar to the process for making straight or skinny pants (page 110). Taper the leg following the pin marks, try on, and re-pin as needed until you like the shape. Then copy on the other leg.

**5.** Also just like you would with the pants, cut off the extra seam allowance from the flared portion, leaving about a ½″ (13mm) seam allowance. However, instead of pinking the edges and pressing the seam open, finish the seam with a serger or with your machine's zigzag stitch.

Press the seam to one side (the same direction it is pressed higher up on the jeans).

**6.** Using denim thread in a matching color to the original jeans trim thread, topstitch the new inseam from the unpicked point down to the future hem.

**7.** Try on the jeans again and mark where you want the hem to be. Measure 1″ (2.5cm) down from that point and cut.

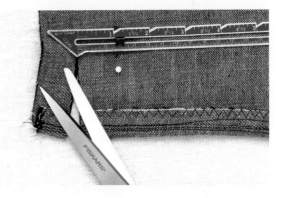

**8.** Press the bottom edge under ½″ (13mm) twice and pin in place. With the top-stitching thread in the bobbin, hem the jeans. (See Hemming, Method 1, page 39.)

# Silky Blouse Makeover

Many variations on the classic silky blouse have become popular in recent years, including color-blocking, contrasting collars or button carriers, high-low hems, and embellished pockets. All of these make great DIY ideas for giving that slightly boring or unflattering blouse in your closet a fun facelift. Here's one technique that turns any blouse with sleeves into a versatile sleeveless top, perfect for layering and using year-round.

You can also try trimming this blouse with a wider bias tape for a bold contrast look. Use double-fold bias tape like the one used in Contrast-Trim Blazer (page 105), or make your own trim out of any light- or medium-weight fabric cut on the bias (see Fabric Terms, page 24), or make it out of the extra fabric from the sleeve of the shirt, as we'll do in the next project (page 122)!

## You Will Need:

- Blouse with sleeves

- Single-fold bias tape, ½″ (13mm) wide, in coordinating color (or contrasting, if you like)

- Standard sewing supplies

# Get It Done

**1.** Carefully trim off the sleeves of the blouse, leaving the serged seam allowance on the body of the shirt.

**2.** Open up the bias tape and find the slightly narrower half. We'll call this the "right" side. Position the right side of the tape against the right side of the blouse. Pin in place around the armhole, beginning at the underarm side seam. At the beginning of the seam, fold the short end of the bias tape over about ⅜″ (9mm) to hide the raw edges. Stitch using a ¼″ (6mm) seam allowance through the fold of the tape. Overlap the ends of the bias tape as you complete the seam.

**3.** Press the bias over the seam allowance and underside of the bias tape, keeping the narrower side of the bias tape folded.

**4.** Fold the bias tape over the raw edges of the armhole along the foldline and pin. It will probably be easiest to keep in place if you pin vertically. (The bias tape may not cover the entire width of the serged seam. That's okay, because it will never show, and the multiple layers of fabric will ensure that the shirt holds up to the weight of the seam you make through the bias tape.)

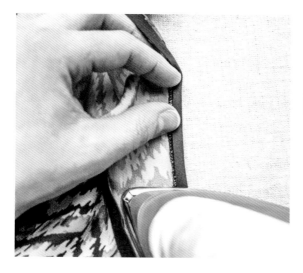

**5.** Topstitch through all layers of the bias tape and blouse. The bias tape will stretch slightly and curve smoothly along the curves of the armholes.

# Tie-Waist Blouse Makeover

For an even more dramatic blouse makeover, you can go much further than just removing the sleeves as in Silky Blouse Makeover (page 118). This transformation also changes the silhouette of a blouse body. Woven cotton shirts are best for this slightly more complicated project, but any basic light- or medium-weight shirt will work. Try it with a checkered blouse for a great vintage 50s look, or work with a soft chambray shirt and a lower waistline for an effortless summer top.

Wear it styled with the ends tied together in a knot for a flirty vibe! This revamp makes for a playful go-anywhere top for a camping trip, a summer BBQ, or relaxing in the sun.

# You Will Need:

- Woven shirt (make sure the armholes aren't deeper than you're comfortable with; looser shirts may have wide armholes that expose your bra band or too much skin)

- Standard sewing supplies

- Fabric pen or chalk *(optional)*

# Get It Done

*Refer to Bias (page 24) for more information.*

**1.** Carefully cut off the sleeves of the shirt, leaving the serged seam allowance on the sleeve side (to reduce bulk on the body side).

**2.** Cut carefully along the center seam of the sleeves, leaving as much fabric intact as possible.

**3.** Press the sleeves flat. The sleeve fabric can be used to cut bias strips for the armhole facing. To start a bias cut, fold back the sleeve at the widest part, matching the grain back on itself above the diagonal fold.

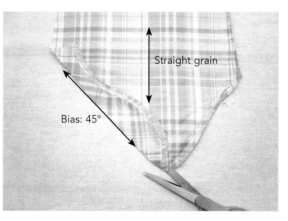

**4.** Using a quilting ruler or hem gauge, cut a 1½″ (3.8cm) strip parallel to the first diagonal bias cut. Mark with a fabric pen or chalk before cutting if you desire. For the next pieces, use the first strip as a pattern. Cut most of the sleeve into 1½″ (3.8cm) strips; they will be approximately the same length until closer to the cuff where the sleeve narrows. You'll need 4–6 bias strips.

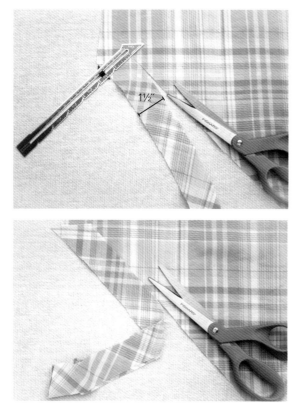

**5.** Following the grainline of the fabric, trim the seam allowances from each bias strip, leaving straight grain ends.

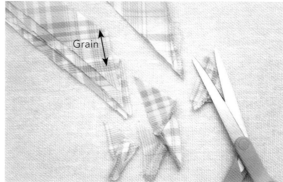

**6.** Sew the bias strips together end to end, with right sides together, using a ½″ (13mm) seam allowance.

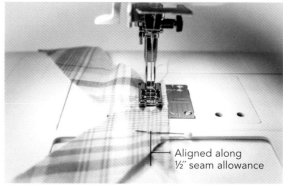

**7.** Press open the seam allowances and trim off the excess triangles.

**8.** Fold under ½″ (13mm) on a side of the bias strip. Use a hem gauge to check that this is ⅓ the width of the strip. Press.

**9.** On the other side of the strip, sew the bias to the shirt armholes with right sides together, beginning at the underarm. Begin stitching ¼″ to ½″ (6–13mm) down from the beginning of the bias strip to allow for folding over. Stitch all along the armhole. As you come back to the starting point, flip the tail of bias from the beginning over on itself. Stitch over the fold about ⅜″ (9mm).

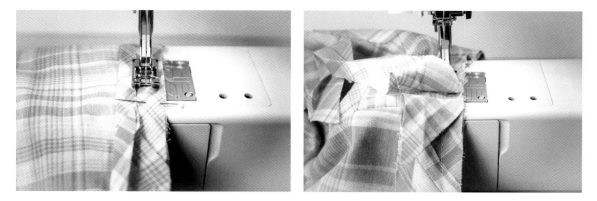

**10.** Trim off the excess bias in the seam allowances.

**11.** Press open the bias binding, keeping the opposite side folded under ½″ (13mm).

**12.** Press the bias strip back onto the body of the shirt and pin. The bias should stretch a little and curve with the arm opening. Sew approximately ⅛″ (3mm) from the edge of the folded edge of the bias. This creates a facing on the armholes and finishes the raw edges you created by cutting off the sleeves. Now you have a sleeveless button-up shirt.

**13.** Try on the shirt and mark where you want it to end, probably a little below your waist. Mark with pins on both sides and at the center back. Fold in half to make sure both sides match. Cut symmetrically from side to side 1″ (2.5cm) below the desired length.

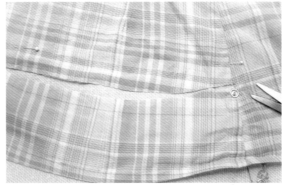

**14.** Using a seam ripper, unpick several inches of the hem on the center front on both sides of the shirt. Press open.

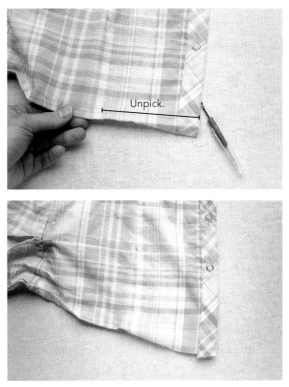

Unpick.

**15.** Cut out the desired tie shape, 1″ (2.5cm) larger than you want the finished tie to be. Use the first side as a pattern for the second side, aligning at the top and bottom of the shirt, for symmetry.

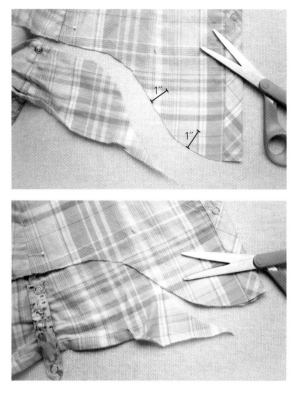

**16.** Refer to Hemming, Method 1 (page 39) for guidance. Fold under ½″ (13mm) all the way around the bottom edge of the shirt and press. Fold up another ½″ (13mm) and press. Pin in place, being careful at the curves. Make tiny pleats if necessary to keep the center fronts and sides aligned straight.

**17.** Sew the hem all the way around.

# Blouse-into-Dress Makeover

Dresses may seem a little too complicated for a beginner sewist, but this one uses a top you already have combined with what I think is the simplest skirt technique ever. Have fun choosing fabric for the skirt that coordinates with your top. Some of my favorite versions are two-tone, with one color for the bodice and a different color or print for the skirt. Casual, fun, and girly!

This project is also a good one for kids' clothes. If a child gets too tall for a favorite tee or top, mark her waistline on it and attach a skirt—trimming the fabric as needed to size down.

Once you master this technique, try a double-layer skirt, like a sheer over a lightweight lining. Or try using a more structured tube top or fitted blouse.

# You Will Need:

To calculate the ideal width for the skirt panel or panels, multiply the waist measurement by a little over 1½. If your waist is between 22″ and 32″ (56cm and 81cm), you should be able to use standard 45″-wide fabric for a comfortable and flattering skirt.

- Woven tank, blouse, or top

- About 1 yard (0.9m) and up to 3 yards (2.7m), depending on length and dress size, of coordinating, pre-washed fabric (slightly heavier fabric recommended, like a lightweight cotton twill, cotton sateen, or linen)

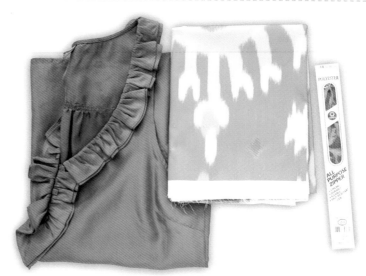

- Coordinating zipper, 12″ (30.5cm) to 18″ (45.5cm)

- Standard sewing supplies

- Fabric pen or chalk *(optional)*

- Pinking shears or serger *(optional)*

# Get It Done

**1.** Try on the top. Insert pins to mark where you want the skirt to begin; typically this is at your natural waist. Lay the top flat and cut at this point all the way around, matching the sides for symmetry first.

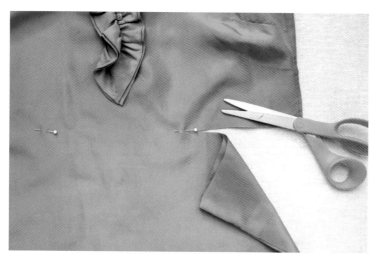

## Note

If you have a large bust or if the shirt does not have any shaping bust darts, cut the front 1″–2″ (2.5–5cm) longer than the back. If you want a blousier top, cut 1″ (2.5cm) longer than the desired waist all around the extra room. If you're not sure, always err on the side of caution and leave some extra length!

**2.** To determine how much fabric to cut for the skirt, hold the fabric up to yourself in a mirror and align the bottom edge where you want it to fall on your legs. Note where the fabric hits your waist, and measure from this point to the bottom of the fabric. Add ½″ (13mm) to this length for the top seam allowance and up to 2½″ (6.5cm) for the hem and hem turn-under. A deep 2″ (5cm) hem will help the skirt fall nicely and give good weight. A heavier fabric might not require such a deep hem. (Refer to Hemming, Method 1, page 39.)

# Note

My skirt piece was 22½″ long including ½″ (13mm) for the top seam allowance and 2½″ (6.3cm) for the hem. Those with larger waists will need twice as much fabric. Cut 2 pieces of fabric of the desired length and trim them both to the width calculated by multiplying your waist measurement by 1½.

**3.** Cut across the fabric at the length you just calculated. With woven fabric, instead of cutting with scissors, you can tear across the fabric—the line will always be straight on grain this way. Snip at the center fold and tear to the selvages.

**4.** To calculate the waistband, measure your waist and add 2″ (5cm). This allows for ½″ (13mm) seam allowances on both ends and 1″ (2.5cm) of wearing ease; you can add more if desired.

**5.** Cut 2 waistband pieces (a piece will be the lining). For a finished 1″ (2.5cm) waistband, cut or tear a 2″ (5cm) strip from the remaining fabric. Repeat for a second piece.

**6.** Mark the center fronts and backs of these pieces by folding them in half. If your skirt has two pieces, mark this fold: you'll need to match the skirt's full side seam to this fold. Mark the ends with a pin ½″ (13mm) from the raw edges, indicating the seamlines for the zipper. Bring the center fold to the pin mark. Snip triangles at the top and bottom edges of the new folds to mark the centers.

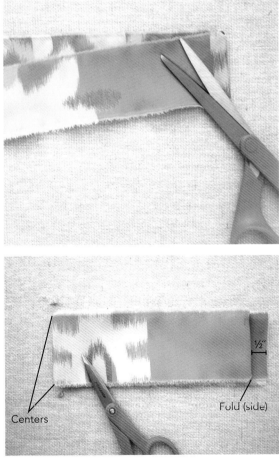

Centers

½″

Fold (side)

**7.** Pin the main skirt fabric right sides together along the selvage or lengthwise edge. Starting about 8″ (20.5cm) down from the top edge (to leave room to insert the zipper), sew with a ½″ (13mm) seam allowance. For those with two skirt pieces, sew the other side seam all the way from waist to hem.

(If you used the entire width of the fabric, you will sew ½″ [13mm] from the selvage edge and so will not have any raw edges inside. If you use less than the full width of the fabric, or if you use multiple panels and have a torn or cut edge along the grain, finish this edge with pinking shears after sewing. If you don't have pinking shears but do have raw edges, you can finish them with a zigzag stitch separately on each side before sewing them together.)

**8.** Press the seam open.

**9.** Fold under ½″ (13mm) all the way around the skirt bottom, measuring with a hem gauge. Press.

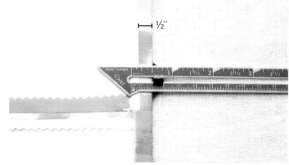

**10.** Fold under another 2″ (5cm) for the hem, press, and pin.

**11.** Refer to Hemming, Method 1 (page 39) for guidance. At the machine, stitch the hem, using a straight stitch as shown or using an invisible hem stitch like the stitch used in Shorten a Pencil Skirt (page 62).

**12.** Gather the top of the skirt. Starting ½″ (13mm) from the seamline, stitch around the entire skirt ⅜″ (9mm) from the edge using a long stitch length and tight upper tension. The fabric will gather automatically. Start and stop stitching ½″ (13mm) away from the edges of the fabric at the side opening.

**13.** Run a gathering stitch all the way around the bottom edge of the bodice, ⅜″ (9mm) from the edge, in the same manner as you gathered the skirt waistline. Using a seam ripper, pick out the original left side seam entirely and press flat. You will use this seam allowance when you sew in the zipper.

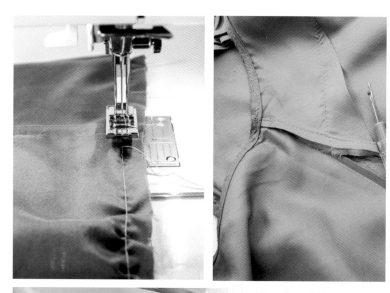

**Tip** To make the long ends of the gathering thread easier to pull on without the risk of pulling them out, tie together both pairs of bobbin threads, knotting them near the ends. Use this loop end as a handle as you pull the threads to make the skirt fit the waistband.

**14.** Match the center front and back of the bodice with a waistband strip, right sides together. The opened left seam of the shirt creates two edges that align with the ends of the waistband. Evenly distribute the gathers and pin.

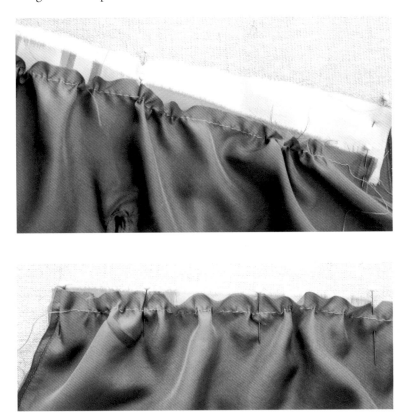

**15.** Switch to regular tension and use a medium-long basting stitch to secure the gathers to the waistband piece, leaving a ⅜" (9mm) seam allowance.

**16.** Pin the second (lining) waistband piece inside the bodice, creating a sandwich with the 2 waistband pieces on the outside and the bodice fabric in between. The wrong sides of the waistband pieces should face out. Sew together all 3 pieces with a regular straight stitch and a ½" (13mm) seam allowance. These stitches should land outside the row of basting stitches.

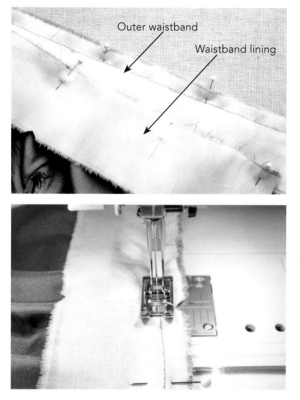

**17.** Press both waistband pieces away from the bodice.

**18.** On the inside (lining) waistband piece, fold up ⅜" (9mm) on the lower edge, using a hem gauge to measure. Press in place.

**19.** Pull the row of gathering thread on the skirt. With the right sides of the skirt facing the right side of the outer waistband, align the center front and back notches of the skirt. The edges of the partially stitched side seam of the skirt align with the ends of the waistband. If your skirt is made from two panels, match the completely stitched side seam to the side fold in the waistband you marked in Step 6. Pin in place.. Distribute the gathers evenly and pin all around. Sew with a ½" (13mm) seam allowance, hiding the gathering row inside the seam allowance.

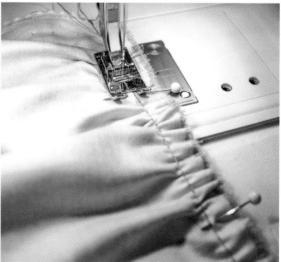

**20.** Press the gathered seam allowance toward the waistband.

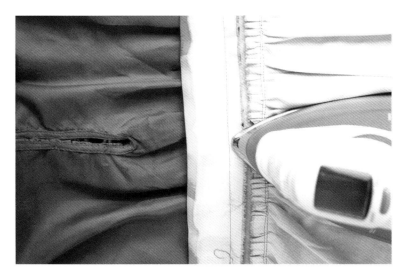

**21.** Fold the lining piece of the waistband back toward the gathering and pin. It should end ⅛″ (3mm) past the bottom seam.

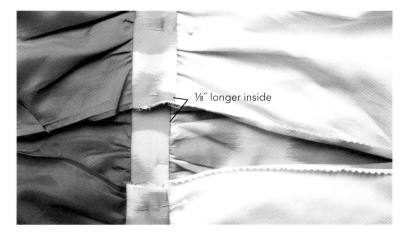

⅛″ longer inside

**22.** Stitch in-the-ditch from the outside of the skirt on the gathered side, securing the waistband lining. Sew along the seam where the gathers meet the waistband edge.

**23.** The following instructions are for a centered zipper, but you can choose to do a lapped zipper (refer to the zipper package for instructions) or use an invisible zipper instead. To insert the zipper: On the left side seam, use a large basting stitch and sew a ½″ (13mm) seam allowance. Sew just beyond the beginning of the skirt seam you made. Press open.

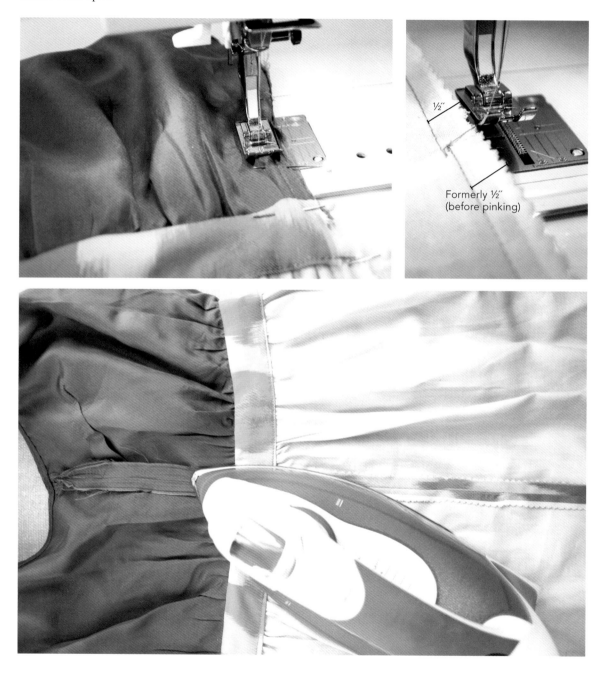

**24.** Center the zipper right side down over the seam. Pin it in place on the left side, aligning the top tabs just below the armhole opening and aligning the zipper pull with the beginning of your basting stitch. With a zipper foot on the machine and still using a long basting stitch, open the zipper and sew it in place to the left side seam allowance.

**25.** Turn right side out. Switch to a regular straight stitch and topstitch, starting in the seamline at the center bottom of the zipper, for 2 or 3 stitches. Pivot with the needle down and follow the seam allowance all the way to the armhole.

**26.** Check that the zipper is still aligned in the center of the seam; if so, start at the center bottom of the zipper on the right side and sew up to the armhole.

**27.** With a seam ripper, carefully unpick the basting stitches holding together the side seam along the length of the zipper. Remove the stray threads.

# Zipper-Shoulder Sweater

I love a long, comfy sweater, but sometimes they're a little too plain. Rather than always adding on accessories, I often like projects that involve a simple, functional embellishment. Metal zippers that are designed to be exposed come in several colors and lengths, so you can have your pick. Choose one that matches—or boldly contrasts with—a plain sweater.

This technique works great on a raglan-sleeve sweater, like the one shown, but you could also add this embellishment on a side seam near the hem of any sweater, or along the shoulder seam of of a basic crewneck with straight shoulder seams.

## You Will Need:

- Pullover sweater (raglan sleeve style recommended to get this look)

- Coordinating zipper, 9″ (23cm) to 11″ (28cm) (slightly shorter than the front shoulder/sleeve seam on your sweater)

- ⅛ yard (12cm) iron-on interfacing close to sweater color

- Zipper foot

- Standard sewing supplies

# Get It Done

**1.** Cut a strip of interfacing approximately the same length and width as the zipper.

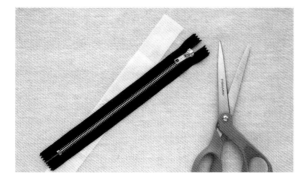

**2.** Turn the sweater inside out and iron the interfacing onto the wrong side of the raglan seam, from the neck band nearly to the underarm side seam. Turn the sweater right side out and trim off the excess interfacing at the curve of the neck edge.

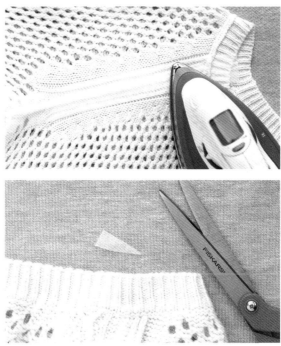

**3.** Line up the top of the zipper pull with the edge of the neck band and center the zipper on the shoulder seam. Pin the zipper in place along both sides. Feel through the layers to ensure the zipper is centered on the bump of the shoulder seam. You may have to curve the zipper slightly at the bottom to keep it centered if the seam curves for the underarm. At the bottom edge of the zipper, turn under the end of the tail and pin in place.

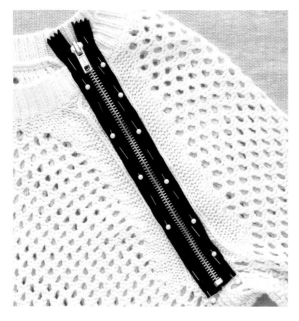

**4.** Starting at the neck edge, sew down either side of the zipper about ⅛″ (3mm) from the teeth, using a zipper foot and removing pins as you work.

**5.** Sew up the second side beginning with the zipper tail and sewing back toward the neck edge with the same ⅛″ (3mm) distance from the zipper teeth.

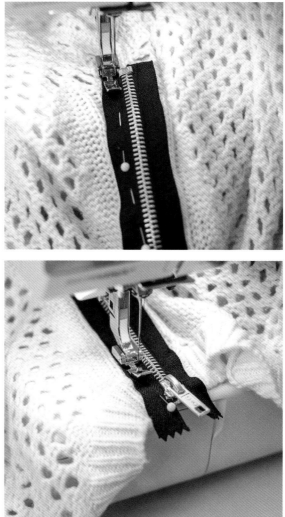

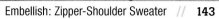

**6.** Switch to a standard sewing machine foot and topstitch along the outer edges of the zipper tape, about ⅛″ (3mm) inside.

**7.** Unzip the zipper. Turn the sweater inside out again and very carefully trim alongside the shoulder seam, between it and the inside edge of stitches on each side. This will remove the bulbous shoulder seam allowance of the sweater. Cut it away beginning just above the bottom end of the zipper.

**8.** Turn the sweater right side out. Switch back to the zipper foot. Fold the top ends of the zipper over the edge of the sweater; pin them down and sew in place.

# Tuxedo-Stripe Pants

I love the look of a tuxedo stripe on pants, particularly on colored or patterned ones! You can combine the colors and materials you want to make your own unique tuxedo pants. Use a bias-cut strip of satin (with the edges pressed under) or lightweight faux leather for a dressier look, or try a colored trim on a dark pair of pants that would work for the office. For the strip, choose something that has a little stretch or give to it, like a bias strip or the twill tape I used.

## You Will Need:

- Pants

- 2 to 2½ yards (1.8–2.3m) contrast trim or finished bias strip (more than double the length of the side seams)

- Standard sewing supplies

# Get It Done

*Refer to Removing Stitches (page 35) for guidance.*

**1.** Using a seam ripper or thread snips, at each side seam, unpick the stitches that secure the waistband facing to the pants. Then unpick the seam securing the waistband to the pants. Do this about 1″–2″ (2.5–5cm) on either side of each side seam.

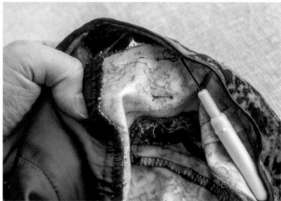

**2.** Align the trim with the side seam of the pants. Because my trim was lightweight and the side seam of my pants was bulky, I lined up the front edge of the trim with the edge of the back pants piece. This allowed me to maintain the size of the pocket opening. Instead, you could center the trim on the side seam if your trim is wide enough to hide the bulk of the side seam and if the pocket opening will still be big enough for your hand. Pin the trim in place.

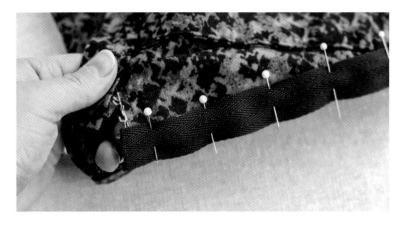

**3.** Slide pants on your machine's free arm and sew along the front ends of the trim, about ⅛" (3mm) from the edge. (For me this meant sewing through the original seam allowance as well). Sew to the bottom of the pant leg and cut the trim, leaving a tail of about 1½" (3.8cm).

**4.** Pin the opposite edge of the trim so that it lies flat and sew ⅛″ (3mm) from that edge, starting again at the waistband of the pants and working down to the hem.

**5.** Fold the cut edge of the trim to the inside of the pant leg, keeping it tight to the hem of the pants, and pin. Sew over the ⅛″ (3mm) seams on both sides of the trim far enough up the leg to hold the tail in place.

**6.** To redo the waistband seams you picked out, pin the waistband to the main pants edge and redo the seam with the original seam allowance, connecting it to the seam where you stopped picking out stitches.

**7.** Pin the facing flat and sew on the outside of the pants directly adjacent to the waistband, hiding the stitches in the fold of the waistband against the pants (stitch in-the-ditch method).

# Boxy Tee Makeover

This is one of the first revamp techniques I taught myself. I kept getting cool lettered tees that were several sizes too large during my college years and I learned to bring them down to size without leaving the shoulder seams in a weird place or causing the sleeves to fit badly. This is a fun and easy way to make just about any tee custom fitted!

I like doing this makeover to make huge tees into a more close-fit, women's style, but you can also create a boxy pajama top or gym tee this way. This project uses a French seam technique similar to the one explained in Infinity Scarf Makeover (page 80). The result is smooth, finished seam allowances on the inside of the tee.

## Note

To simply take in the side seams of a sweater or tee that is a little loose in the waist, refer to Take In a Sweater or Knit Top (page 46).

## You Will Need:

- Loose, boxy tee

- Perfectly fitted tee to use as a pattern

- Standard sewing supplies

- Walking foot (recommended)

- Double needle (recommended)

- Fabric pen or chalk (*optional*)

# Get It Done

*For additional details on how to sew a French seam, refer to Infinity Scarf Makeover (page 80).*

**1.** Fold both tees in half lengthwise. Pin the necks and hems at the fold line to mark the centers. Place the loose tee on a flat surface. Place the fitted tee (the pattern) on top, aligning centers. Cut the loose tee along the sides, leaving ⅝″–1″ (1.5–2.5cm) for a seam allowance, depending on the relative stretch of both tees (the less stretch in the fabric of the loose tee, the more wearing ease you'll need). You can trace these lines with a fabric pen or chalk before you cut if you're worried about keeping both pieces symmetrical.

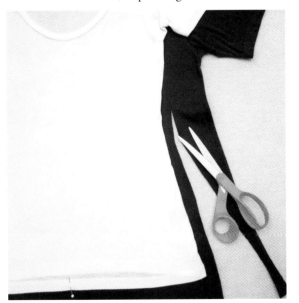
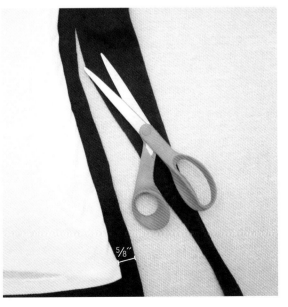

**2.** Flip back the sleeve of the pattern tee so you can see the curve of its arm opening. Follow this curve at the armhole as you cut the loose tee, cutting off the sleeve and leaving approximately a ½″ (13mm) seam allowance.

**3.** Repeat on the other side, or use the first side as a pattern for the second side. Fold tee in half lengthwise to check that both sides are symmetrical. You may have to trim off some excess on a side.

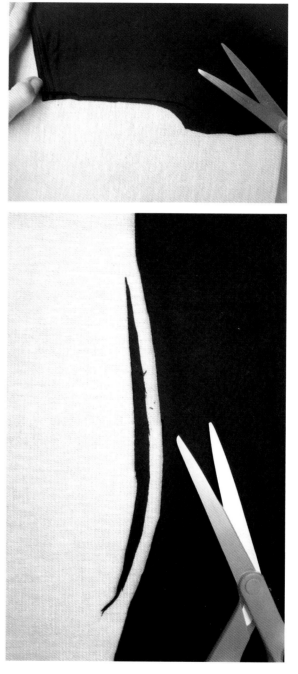

**4.** Use the fitted tee as a sleeve pattern. Match the shoulder seams. Again, leave room for a ⅝″–1″ (1.5cm–2.5cm) seam allowance.

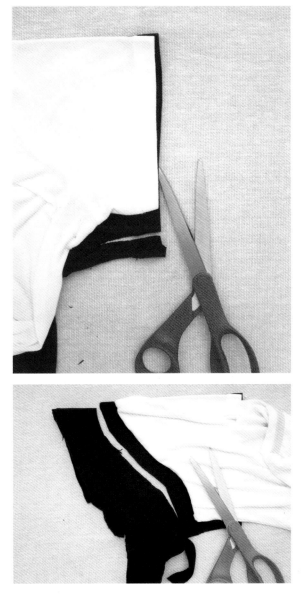

**5.** At the machine, begin the French seams on the side seams. With wrong sides together, stitch from the hem to the armhole, leaving a ¼″ (6mm) seam allowance.

**6.** Reassemble the sleeves with French seams, first sewing with wrong sides together and a ¼″ (6mm) seam allowance.

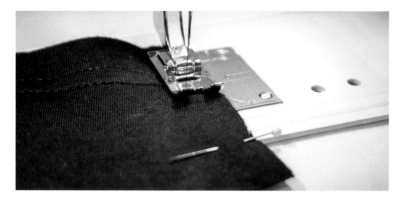

**7.** Press the new seam allowances to the side, and then flip over and press from the outside. Then, with right sides together, fold the tee in half and press flat with the seam at the center of the fold. Center the seam along the new folded edge, and pin through the seam allowance to keep it in place. Do this on the sleeves as well.

**8.** Using a ⅜″ (9mm) seam allowance, sew along the entire length of the side seams and sleeve seams, tucking the ¼″ (6mm) seam allowance inside the seam. This way, there will be no raw edges on the long seams of the tee.

**9.** Turn the sleeves right side out and tuck them into the inside-out tee, aligning the shoulder folds and sleeve seams. Sew to the armholes with ½″ (13mm) seam allowances. Finish these seam allowances with a zigzag stitch on the edge.

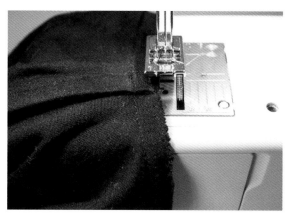

**10.** Try on the tee for length. If you're pleased, you're done! If it's too long now that it fits snugly, mark with pins your desired length. Cut across the tee 1″ (5cm) below this point. Use a straightedge to make sure it is even all the way around.

**11.** Press under a 1″ (2.5cm) hem, and pin. Refer to Hemming, Method 3 (page 40).

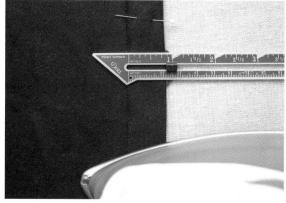

**12.** With a double needle and 2 matching spools of thread, still using a walking foot to prevent stretching, hem the shirt close to the cut edge on the underside of the hem. The narrow zigzag on the inside of the hem will finish the raw edge of the tee.

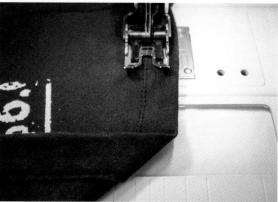

# (Nearly) Unlimited Embellishment Ideas

With a can-do DIY attitude and sewing and alteration skills, you can make over as many items of clothing as you want using the methods in *DIY Wardrobe Makeovers*.

Don't let your creativity and self-expression end with the projects in this book. There are so many possible options for DIY upgrades to your clothes, it's impossible to describe them all! Think of the combinations you can put together using the tees, tanks, sweaters, sweatshirts, skirts, dresses, jeans, and pants already in your closet or dresser.

While many of the projects presented are specific to a particular type of garment, any item you own can be made more personal with a little embellishment or customization. Check out these additional ideas. I like to imagine how I could add a favorite shape or texture to any of the items in my closet! Keep an eye out for embellishments.

## Embellishments

Lace

**Braid trim**, such as for home decor (I love pom-pom braid and sequin braid)

**Leather scraps** or fake leather or fur

**Store-bought appliqués** or patches

**Homemade appliqués**, using fabric and iron-on adhesive (like the Elbow Patch Sweater Makeover, page 92, and Riding Pants Makeover, page 96)

**Just about anything you can sew through!**

Don't let your creativity and self-expression end with the projects in this book.

## Garments You Can Embellish

Tanks   Tees   Sweatshirts   Hoodies   Shorts   Skirts   Hats

# Resources

It can be hard to know where to look when you're starting out sewing and making your own clothes. I'm lucky to have some great local fabric stores near me, and I love to find fabric and notions at thrift stores and vintage shops. Here are some great online resources available to you no matter where you live.

**Kollabora** // is an online community and store full of all kinds of sewing inspiration and tools. Many of the tools and materials used in this book were provided by Kollabora, and you can purchase them all on Kollabora.com.

**Spoonflower** // For a truly one-of-a-kind DIY clothing project, the options are seriously unlimited with Spoonflower, an online service that lets you upload an image and turn it into fabric. I love that it has so many good choices for fabric weight and content options, too, beyond the basic quilting cotton (I love the twill, organic cotton knit, and cotton sateen). Spoonflower.com

**Bernina USA** // Bernina lent me the 350PE machine you see in this book, and it's a great one for the basic garment and home decor sewing I do. It's a very high-quality machine, with all the features I need but no unnecessary bells and whistles. All the extra machine parts used in this book are also from Bernina, and you can get them at your local Bernina retailer; find your local store at Bernina.com.

# About the Author

Suzannah Hamlin Stanley has been sewing since she was a child and has been writing about her projects on her blog, *Create/Enjoy* (formerly *Adventures in Dressmaking*), since 2009. She has made everything from knit tops to living room curtains to tote bags and her own wedding dress, and she loves to make practical, usable items for her wardrobe and home.

A DIYer at heart, Suzannah has a do-it-yourself attitude about home decorating, cooking from scratch, natural beauty products, and all kinds of other pursuits. She lives with her husband outside Portland, Oregon.